6/11/11

To: Eric
With love

MARRIAGE

◇

Under Construction

for Men

ANGELA CASTILLO HERNANDEZ

LUIS HERNANDEZ

DEDICATION

We dedicate this book to our parents, Miguel and Evelyn Castillo, and Irma Negron, for the years devoted to raising us with their best efforts and instilling values of love, family and relationship. We also dedicate this book to our other close family and friends who have shared life with us. But, a special dedication goes to four wonderful men who are no longer with us, but were examples in our lives, in honor, respect, but above all, love. They are Hipolito Millet, Julio Castillo, Rogelio Nazario, and Pedro Feliciano.

CONTENTS

ACKNOWLEDGMENTS

First and foremost, we thank God for this amazing opportunity to touch marriages, and for the years of faithfulness in our lives. We thank Amy McClintock for her advice and insight as to how even to begin this project. She selflessly shared information just for the sake of helping. We also thank Jasmin Almodovar for her obedience in sharing with us the vision and word the Lord gave her, that we should begin the writing. We give a special thank you to our coach and editor of this project, Jane Fisher. She is truly an exceptional woman who is dedicated and cares about this work as though it was her own. Her insight and advice throughout this journey has been of great value. We could not have done this without her.

PREFACE

Thank you for choosing Marriage Under Construction! The book you have in your hands began as our notes for the marriage conference we present through Remodel Ministries. It has since grown to be both the conference guide for the attendees and a standalone book. We are amazed and humbled at how the Lord would use us in this fashion to touch the lives of so many people.

Although you will note that Angela speaks in the first person throughout the book, we wrote this book together as a couple, identifying the things the Lord has taught us through our 20 plus years of marriage. The book is written in the same casual tone used in the live conference, so that as far as possible, you have the feeling of being there with us.

There are two versions of the book, one for women and the other for men. Four of the chapters are the same in each book, which reflects the presentation of this material to the couples at the marriage conference. The purpose of the conference is to help couples grow closer together, and this is facilitated by receiving and discussing the information together.

In the third and fifth chapters, however, Luis speaks directly to men only, and Angela speaks directly to women only, again reflecting the marriage conference. The conference's split sessions allow husbands and wives an opportunity to speak candidly with only other men, or only other women, about the challenges and responsibilities of their different roles in the marriage.

This book is appropriate for individual or small group study, as well as a conference guide. Workbook pages are included, with both challenge questions based on the content written, and with many of the specific Bible verses that support the material. We encourage you to study the passages, and space is provided for notations.

We hope you will grow spiritually through these books, and pray for God's special blessings in your marriage.

Luis & Angela

Chapter One

BLUEPRINT

...whose architect and builder is God.
Hebrews 11:10, NIV

I was nineteen years old when Luis and I were married. I really had no idea what I was in store for. I saw what my parents' marriage looked like. I saw what the marriages of my relatives, family friends and couples from the church looked like. However, I really had no idea what marriage was. I was like every other young woman who dreamed of getting married to "The One." I only imagined being loved and taken care of.

My husband and I met and married in five months. We eloped, and we were so in love that we wanted nothing more than to spend our lives together. I thought we knew everything, and knew all we needed to know at that time. I wasn't prepared for what was coming next.

The Dream Becomes Reality

Shortly after marrying my husband, I realized that there was a lot more to marriage than I understood. I knew there would be disputes and difficulties. Nevertheless, I always assumed that it would be easy to navigate through, as long as there was enough love. I was wrong.

It wasn't easy, even with all the love I felt. There was difficulty in adjusting to my new life. I now had new responsibilities to take care of him. In addition to working and attending school, I had to cook, clean, do the laundry, take care of our children, and make sure that he had what he needed on a daily basis. I had to think about what he liked, and what he wanted. It was no longer just about me. I had to consider his thoughts and his preferences.

In the beginning, this wasn't a problem. In fact, I was so in love that I looked forward to doing things for him. I looked forward to pleasing him and doing my best to make him happy. But, as time passed and disagreements set in, it wasn't so easy to do at times. It was difficult because after an argument or a dispute, I honestly didn't want to do anything for him. I really lacked motivation, especially in times when I felt disappointed that he wasn't doing things for me.

As a husband, Luis had similar feelings. He was responsible for more than just himself now and had to take care of me as well.

List the things that you did to demonstrate your love for your spouse when you first got together. Do you still do any of these things today?

When we first started dating, he made every effort to impress me. He took pride in showing me how great of a man he was, and how much he could do for me. When disagreements began, he was less than motivated, just as I had been. I had disappointed him, too.

We quickly learned to be careful with what we said. Things that were never an issue before would stir up an argument. We were arguing about everything. It was frustrating because it didn't matter how small and ridiculous the issue was. We sought advice from my aunt or from our Pastor, and one of the things that we were advised, and knew the Bible said, was not to go to bed angry.

Let me just tell you that when we are angry or upset about something that one of us has done, we are not in the mood to fix anything, let alone sleep so nestled and cuddly with each other. We both had difficulty giving in and we both thought we were right. We each thought it was up to the other to apologize.

I felt that he was not meeting my expectations of what our marriage should be like. I thought, *How could he hurt me if he said he loves me? Doesn't he understand me? Doesn't he know what I expected of him? I haven't changed; I'm still the same person he dated. Is he oblivious? Why can't I do anything right?*

His thoughts were similar. *How could she say she loves me and not respect me? Doesn't she see all the sacrifices I am making? Doesn't she see how hard I am working for our family? I am a good, providing, and hard-working man. Doesn't she see that? What changed? She wasn't like this before.*

How have some of your expectations hurt your spouse?

...Do not let the sun go down while you are still angry, and do not give the devil a foothold.

Ephesians 4:26--27, NIV

We had issues with our families as well. I not only had to deal with all of his issues, but now I had to deal with his family, and he had to deal with mine. I loved his family, and he loved mine, but sometimes it seemed as though we both had too many things to prove to them. *Wasn't it enough that we chose to leave our families to start our own family? Didn't his family see my sacrifice; didn't my family see his?* All we both could think of was, *How could everything be so difficult after it was so great? Did we make a mistake?*

I felt trapped because I knew how the Lord felt about divorce. I did not want to have a failed marriage. What would that say to my family who believed in marriage? What would I tell our children?

I didn't have a dream of a failed marriage. I dreamed of happily ever after. I dreamed of celebrating 25 years, then 50 years of wedded bliss. Although I didn't want to have a failed marriage, I had conflicting information. The information I thought I knew through my religious beliefs, and views of marriage through examples, was different from information I knew the world was providing.

Luis did not have many examples of what marriage should be. In fact, in the beginning he thought that it was a valid option just to walk away from me. However, after Luis accepted Jesus Christ as his Lord and Savior, he also now knew what the Bible had to say and struggled with the same conflict.

The Miracle

Luis accepted the Lord after we faced one of the toughest moments in our life. Our first-born suffered an accident to his head and almost died at 5 months, due to internal bleeding. He survived, thankfully, but later that year he began to have seizures, and it was seriously out of control.

One day at home, after only arriving less than 20 minutes from being discharged from the hospital for his seizures, my son suffered another bad seizure. All we could do was hold him, watch him and wait for the seizure to pass, with prayers that this seizure would not be the one that would cause physical and permanent damage to his brain.

My husband, with tears in his eyes, looked at me and said, "What can we do so that this doesn't continue to happen to him?" In an instant, without even thinking about it, and with true conviction in my heart, I said, "You must accept the Lord Jesus Christ as your Savior, and I must ask for forgiveness and reconcile my life back to Him!"

That night, God gave a miracle in the life of my son. When I returned to the hospital, I prayed by his bedside. That night I gave my heart to the Lord. I pleaded with God to heal my son. I told God that I would serve Him no matter what, if He healed my son, or even if He didn't. I said I was sorry for turning my back on Him for so many years. I gave my heart to the Lord and was determined to serve Him no matter what happened.

The next day, all sorts of tests were performed in order to find an imbalance in his head. The doctors had diagnosed him with epilepsy. They had to run multiple tests to find out what specifically was happening to him. The test results came back, and what happened next was astonishing.

I was taken to a conference room filled with about eight doctors. They were all discussing my son's case. They were baffled because they couldn't understand why all the test results came back negative, with no signs of epilepsy. In my heart, I immediately knew what God had done.

The Problem

The next available Sunday we both gave our hearts to the Lord. We were both so grateful and had so much faith in who God is, because of what He did in our son's life. Now we wanted to make sure we obeyed Him in every aspect in our lives, including our marriage. However, it doesn't mean that it was any easier to deal with, or to do. So now, Luis faced my same dilemma.

Luis didn't grow up with his dad and did not want that for his children. He didn't want his children to feel the void he felt as a child. His father's example was always present in his mind, as well as what he learned in the Word of God. So, we both struggled with the contrasting information between what the world said, and what the Bible taught about marriage.

You may be asking yourself, *What does she mean by "the world's view?" Who is "the world?"* When I talk about the world, I mean general society. A general society that doesn't follow what the Bible has to say, but follows the opinions and beliefs that are formed by a matter of opinion of the general population. In other words, in today's society, what is popular in the public eye or mainstream. Opinions about marriage that are contrary to God's Word have become popular view. You must make sure not to fall into those thoughts so that you're not led down the wrong path.

Something very popular to say is, "You only live once." Some other common clichés and well-known quotes are:

> *All life is an experiment. The more experiments you make the better.*
> —Ralph Waldo Emerson

> *If you obey all the rules, you'll miss all the fun.*
> —Katherine Hepburn

> *There is only one success, to be able to spend your life in your own way.*
> —Christopher Morley

> *Life has no limitations, except the ones you make.*
> —Les Brown

Most people believe these sayings, and see no harm in them. However, if you look closer you can see from these common clichés, the view of the world is *self-gratification.* In this technologically enhanced era people want things bigger, bolder, better and faster. If it's not fast enough, self-indulgent enough, the best, or the biggest, then it's no good. Therefore, when I say "the world" you can now understand that I mean what is popular to the general population. These thoughts are contrary to what the Word of God says. The Word of God speaks about self-gratification in this way:

> *He died for everyone so that those who receive his new life will no longer live for themselves. Instead, they will live for Christ, who died and was raised for them.*
>
> **2 Corinthians 5:15 (NLT)**

What some may not understand is that we, as followers of Christ, believe that we should die to self and live for God. The world does not view this in the same way, but promotes the opposite, as you can tell from the common clichés mentioned. You can see it every day on television, in movies, in mainstream media and in other ways. However, the world doesn't come up with all these lies and thoughts on their own. Lies originate from Satan.

Describe what you've been taught about marriage and relationships from others and popular opinion.

_____

_____

_____

_____

_____

_____

_____

_____

_____

_____

_____

_____

_____

_____

_____

_____

_____

Don't let anyone capture you with empty philosophies and high-sounding nonsense that come from human thinking and from the spiritual powers of this world, rather than from Christ.
Colossians 2:8 (NLT)

For the word of the Lord is right and true...
Psalms 33:4, NIV

...your word is truth.
John 17:17, NIV

Satan deceives the hearts and minds of people and infiltrates the world with these lies.

What do I mean by "lies" of Satan? The Word of God is truth, therefore anything contrary to the Word of God is false or a lie. Satan formulates all lies, then he uses these lies to confuse our thoughts, and then it becomes part of the thoughts of society. You see an example of this in the Garden of Eden. When Satan approached Eve in the Garden, he lied to get her attention, and then continued to lie in order to confuse her and convince her.

> *Now the serpent was more crafty than any of the wild animals the Lord God had made. He said to the woman, "Did God really say, 'You must not eat from any tree in the garden'?"*
>
> **Genesis 3:1, NIV**

God didn't say that they must not eat from *any* tree. God specifically said from one very specific tree. So specific that He pointed the tree out by name.

> *And the Lord God commanded the man, "You are free to eat from any tree in the garden; but you must not eat from the tree of the knowledge of good and evil, for when you eat from it you will certainly die."*
>
> **Genesis 2:16—17, NIV**

What are some of the things you have learned from the Word of God concerning marriage.

_____

_____

_____

_____

_____

_____

_____

_____

_____

_____

_____

...He [Satan] has always hated the truth, because there is no truth in him. When he lies, it is consistent with his character; for he is a liar and the father of lies.

John 8:44, NLT

Satan wanted to capture Eve's attention. He wanted to make the fruit of the tree appealing to her, in order to distract her from the truth, so that she and Adam eventually would sin and be separated from God.

Satan has been doing the same ever since. He lies to us in order to make things that are against God's Word seem appealing. He does this so that he can keep us separated from God's truth. His lies infiltrate into the thoughts of people who then feed the views of the world.

The World's View on Marriage

The world has much to say about knowing who your soulmate is, and what marriage should be. You're told that if your spouse doesn't live up to your expectations, then he or she must not be your real soulmate. The world tells you that you can abandon your spouse if you're not satisfied. The world's view of marriage is selfish, which makes the bond weak, powerless, and destructible.

When I speak with some people I know, who do not know the Lord, their mentality is that if your spouse is not fulfilling your desires, or your demands, or doing their part, then that person is a waste of your time. They'll tell you that he or she isn't the one for you because if they were, you wouldn't have so many struggles, they would understand who you are, and it would be much easier.

List any unrealistic expectations that you may have for your spouse.

_____

_____

_____

_____

_____

_____

_____

_____

_____

_____

_____

_____

_____

_____

_____

_____

In fact, they'll tell you, it is a waste of your time and you are too valuable to put up with anything less than what you deserve.

Watching old movies and television shows, if someone was about to get married, it would be for life. If they were in love with someone else, they would sort it out before they got married. Nowadays, there's no pressure to get it right ahead of time because divorce is acceptable now. Today's movies, television shows, and reality TV send the message that it is alright to get divorced.

The world feeds you this thought when entering marriage, "If it doesn't work out, you can just get a divorce." These types of thoughts contribute to many marriages that fail. From the beginning, some may be entering the marriage with an escape plan. Even if someone enters marriage believing that the marriage will be for life, as I did, the moment things were not going your way, the thought of divorce enters your mind. These thoughts entered my mind, not because I wanted divorce, but because I thought that things were so bad, that it was an option.

This thought process stems from selfishness. This isn't something that we can avoid completely. Unfortunately, we are imperfect humans and it's in our nature to be selfish. The main problem is sin. When Adam and Eve sinned, our communication with God and with each other was compromised. We'll discuss in further detail the ramifications of this in another session. However, the point here is that we are naturally selfish beings, and must try our best not to be that way.

The problem with fighting off selfishness is that it is contrary to the behaviors and thought processes that society promotes. Selfishness leads to disappointment, rejection, disapproval, anger, bitterness, isolation, and ultimately to marital destruction. This is mainly because there are two people in a marriage, which leaves no room for selfish desires of one person. Not to ignore what your feelings and desires might be, but you must take into consideration another person, because now you share a life together.

This notion of finding the "one" or our "soulmate" is a myth. People selfishly searching for someone who is perfect for them, increases their expectations, which leads to many disappointments.

What to do Instead

Instead, you should seek the Lord's wisdom as to whom you should marry. Even then, it's impossible completely to avoid troubles with the person you marry. You can vet that person, spend time and properly plan, pray and seek wisdom before the wedding, and still have troubles, and at times feel as though you may have made a mistake. Expect that when you start to think that the person you married is not the right one, the enemy will use that to develop more thoughts of negativity toward your mate and your marriage. This is when it's essential that you understand that your troubles are not necessarily because you didn't find your perfect match.

Who's Your Soulmate?

Both partners in the marriage must work through the issues. You made a commitment to each other, before God, to give your entire self to the marriage. The woman becomes the one the husband must fight for; the man becomes the one the wife must fight for.

So don't think of marriage as finding someone who will be right for you. Approach marriage with the mindset that you'll do whatever you can to be right for your partner. And in the process, you will find that you don't marry the one. The person you marry *becomes* the one.

If you already read the Bible, you know that God tells His plan for how marriage should work. You do your best to work through any problems in your marriages, according to this plan.

There are those who accept the Lord after they marry, even though their spouse has not. The enemy tries to attack that marriage putting thoughts like these as well, using thoughts that he or she is not a believer and therefore now maybe there is an out. The Word tells us to honor these marriages if our spouse is willing.

Of course, there are some who try hard for their marriage, and it still doesn't work out. This could be for many reasons, and there is no condemnation to them. The reasons are between them and God. If they put their life in the Lord's hands and seek His will,

What are the ways you can show your spouse that you are fighting for your marriage?

_____

_____

_____

_____

_____

_____

_____

_____

_____

_____

For the unbelieving husband has been sanctified through his wife, and the unbelieving wife has been sanctified through her believing husband. Otherwise, your children would be unclean, but as it is, they are holy. But if the unbeliever leaves, let I be so. The brother or the sister is not bound in such circumstances; God has called us to live in peace.

1 Corinthians 7:14—15, NIV

God will bring fullness into their life in the manner that He knows is best and perfect for them. He loves them and desires nothing but the best for them.

My point here is to focus on those of you who want to work in your marriages today, and have a chance to strengthen or even save your marriage. About 33% of all marriages currently end in divorce[1] and that is only counting the people who actually got married legitimately. Imagine the amount of couples that live together for years as a marriage (not counted part of this study), and then split up. Although they weren't married legally, had they been, it would count as a divorce.

The world feeds you the idea that somehow if you didn't marry your soulmate, that it's alright to leave and continue searching. However, if you choose to believe with all your heart that the person you married *becomes* your soulmate - that they are the one person who is meant for you - you will work hard to save your marriage.

You'll work hard to ensure that you don't lose your spouse because you know that for you, there is no other one than he or she. The premise that if your partner doesn't meet your expectations, then it means that they aren't the right one after all, is

---

[1] Barna Group, Ventura, CA. (2008, March 31). *New Marriage and Divorce Statistics Released.* Retrieved August 03, 2016, from Barna: https://www.barna.org/barna-update/family-kids/42-new-marriage-and-divorce-statistics-released#.V6IQ8_krKCg

Describe ways that you can show your spouse that your marriage is important to you.

...A wife must not separate from her husband. But if she does, she must remain unmarried or else be reconciled to her husband. And a husband must not divorce his wife.

1 Corinthians 7:10-11 (NIV)

one of the many lies that Satan has filtered into the world, and it has ultimately influenced the church.

50/50

Another misconception is that marriage is a 50/50 proposition. I know this proposition all too well. When my husband and I were first married, we both did our best to please one another. In fact, part of the reason why we wanted to be together was because of how much we did for each other. To each of us, it showed how much we mattered to the other person. I remember thinking, "Wow! He is so sweet, so kind, and would do anything for me." He had me hooked! When we first dated, we were practically kids. I was only 19, and he was 22. We were both young and inexperienced, but thought we knew it all. We thought we had everything figured out.

Shortly after we were married, reality started to set in. We both had the desire to please one another, but it was impossible to do all the time. Then children and responsibilities of work and the house started to set in, and all of a sudden, we had less time with each other. We were tired from everyday life and responsibilities and had no desire to also, then do for one another. We started to argue about who did what, and who did not. Who did more, and who did less. We began to measure each other up. We began to try to keep track of how much we were giving to the relationship, and

Have you thought about the 50/50 concept in your marriage? What are things you have stopped doing that you used to do when you first got together?

_____

_____

_____

_____

_____

_____

_____

_____

_____

_____

_____

_____

_____

Serve wholeheartedly, as if you were servicing the Lord, not people,

Ephesians 6:7, NIV

how little we thought the other was contributing. We began to argue that the other partner wasn't giving their full 50%.

The problem with this notion is that it's not really possible to measure someone else's amount of effort. How do you know when the person has done their 50%? You shouldn't be measuring what the other person is giving, but instead focus on your own contribution to the marriage. In marriage, each person should give 100% without trying to measure what the other is giving. This is true even when one spouse is doing all the giving. How so?

You should be doing everything as though you are doing it for the Lord. You should be investing all your efforts into your marriage. I know it can be difficult sometimes, especially when you feel that your spouse is being particularly difficult. However, this is what the Lord commands us to do. The beautiful thing about this is that when you are obedient to God, even when it's hard, God will honor you for your actions.

Fix Yourself

One beautiful way the Lord may honor you in this, is that He will work in the heart of your spouse. If you look deeper into Colossians 3:23-24 (page 25), it states that you will get a reward from the Lord and He will give you what you should receive. If you combine this with the premise that you will reap what you sow

Do you find that you do things for your spouse out of obligation, or do you do them because you're pleased to do so?

_____

_____

_____

_____

_____

_____

_____

_____

_____

_____

_____

_____

_____

_____

Whatever work you do, do it with all your heart. Do it for the Lord and not for men. Remember that you will get your reward from the Lord. He will give you what you should receive. You are working for the Lord Christ.

Colossians 3:23—24, NLV

(Galatians 6:7), you can infer that as you honor the Lord with your obedience and invest all your efforts into the marriage, you will reap the reward of the Lord working in your spouse. Your focus should be on yourself and doing your very best and the Lord will take care of all the rest.

It is not your job to change your spouse. Actually, didn't you marry your spouse for who they were, defects and all? Yes, you did. Are you perfect? No, you are not.

My assumption is that you thought your spouse was the greatest, and you wanted nothing more but to be with him or her. You dreamed about building a life together. But, when things start getting difficult, you can forget. I forgot. I forgot why I wanted to be with my husband. All of a sudden, I started to see all of his faults. I questioned myself as to why I didn't notice before. Thankfully, God revealed to me that I was not all that perfect. I had many flaws of my own, as Luis was discovering. I was so wrapped up in what I thought I deserved from him—what I needed and what I wanted—that I forgot about *him*.

You can sometimes be so immersed in the world's view, believing that you somehow deserve to receive everything you want, that you give your spouse the job to fulfill your every wish. That type of thinking is grossly inappropriate. How could you expect a simple human to fulfill your every desire and your every need? That would be unreasonable. Ask yourself, do you have the ability to do that for your spouse? I am sure that you will find that

List some reasons why you fell in love with your spouse.

you do not, and you shouldn't expect that from your spouse. The only one who can fill our every need is the Lord. Instead of doing for your spouse only if he or she is living up to their 50%, try always giving 100%. Anything else is selfish ambition.

What's Important

You are to value your spouse, and to serve your spouse not *selfishly*, but *selflessly*. Imagine the impact on your marriage if each of you had this type of attitude? If you would put the interests of your spouse above your own? You would see his or her dedication to the marriage, and it would inspire each of you to do more for each other. If only one of you starts at first, you can still motivate your spouse to give 100%, if you are leading by example.

Selfishness robs the marriage of communication, relationship, intimacy and romance, and leads to weakness. It wasn't easy for me to grasp this concept. Actually, it was quite difficult. I knew I had to serve my husband. Even though I didn't want to, or think he deserved it. I had to put my selfish desires aside and put him first. *Was this always easy to do?* No. It was not. In fact, I failed miserably many times, but had to stay strong and always try.

Luis also tried, but at first, I couldn't see what he was doing, because I was so focused on my own needs, and was looking for specific behavior changes.

What can you do for your spouse to make their day better?

_____

_____

_____

_____

_____

_____

_____

_____

_____

_____

_____

_____

_____

Do nothing out of selfish ambition or vain conceit. Rather, in humility value others above yourselves, not looking to your own interests but each of you to the interests of the others.

Philippians 2:3—4, NIV

I remember praying and seeking the Lord's guidance. In that prayer, I did a lot of complaining. I complained about everything I was doing; I complained about all that Luis was not doing. I wondered when God was going to finally step in.

Then one morning, there was a prayer union in my church. I was on my way to work, but decided to go there instead to pray for my marriage. As I was arriving, I looked up and there was my husband and my best friend arriving to the church as well. He had asked her for advice on what he could do to better our marriage, and showed up to the church to pray for me and our marriage. I was so surprised and filled with so much joy, that I cried. Throughout the time I was selfishly complaining, my husband was actually trying in his own way.

I didn't notice at first, but that day God confirmed to me that He was working in Luis, and I had to be patient. He confirmed that I was not perfect, and He had to do changes in me, as well.

What I also learned was that the same way God loves me, God loves my husband, and that He will do what is best for both of us, if we both trust in Him. I was so focused on my own needs that I forgot that Luis had needs as well. Luis saw my dedication, but I failed to see his. Through prayer and seeking God's guidance, I was able to hear God's voice that morning so that He could confirm all that He was doing for me. It is very easy to feel depressed or get down if you're not careful. You must pray and ask for God's wisdom and strength, and that he will give you courage.

Focusing on our own needs could make us under-appreciate our spouse and cause sadness or make us feel weak. Satan could attack this time with various types of temptation. Write a prayer that can help you get through it.

Watch and pray so that you will not fall into temptation. The spirit is willing, but the flesh is weak.

Matthew 26:41, NIV

Thankfully, I knew the Lord, and through years of praying, years of devotion, years of studying His Word, years of drawing closer to the Lord, and years of working through mistakes and seeking wisdom concerning marriage, I was able to understand God's plan for marriage. His design. His purpose.

This took time to know, and it took devotion and willpower to fight for my marriage, and to fight to do what was right in God's eyes. In order to do that, I had to draw closer to Him. I had to understand first God's design for marriage. I had to put aside my dreams and societal beliefs of what marriage is and what it is not. I also had to put aside societal theories of why marriages fail or why some marriages were not meant to be. I had to look at what God said marriage is supposed to be. Then I had to accept that my marriage was not reflecting God's design, and decide that I needed to do everything in my power to change that.

God's Plan & Purpose

My marriage had to go *under construction*. I had to go back to the drawing board. What happens when you have a construction project? When you begin a project or "go back to the drawing board," you have to start out by drawing up the designs. You have to begin with blueprints.

When I decided to let my marriage go under construction, I had to allow God's blueprint and design to be reflected in my marriage. In order to do that, I had to allow God to enter into *all* areas of my life and my marriage. I had to allow Him to show me what *His* design was, and allow Him to be the Architect of my life, my marriage, and my family.

So what exactly does it mean when I say God's blueprint and design? God's blueprint and design is His purpose and plan for marriage. The Bible illustrates God's purpose and plan for marriage this way:

> *As the Scriptures say, " A man leaves his father and mother and is joined to his wife, and the two are united into one." This is a great mystery, but it is an illustration of the way Christ and the church are one.*
>
> **Ephesians 5:31—32, NLT**

God planned for man and woman to be united into one flesh. They are to leave their parents to build a life together. If you think about how deep this is, you will understand how great this is. Your parents gave you life. They nurtured and cared for you. They taught you and prepared you. In other words, they provided such a big service to you so that you could become the adults you need to be. Even after all of this, God says to leave them. God says to leave them in order to be married, in order to form a new family.

The parents He said to honor are the ones you must leave, and now your focus should be your spouse. Not that you should ever stop honoring your parents. But, now you have a covenant with your spouse. The Word of God states that this is a great mystery and compares it to the way Christ and the church are one. Christ has a covenant with you, and you have a covenant with your spouse. A covenant is an agreement, a contract, and a bond. This is a great testimony to what a true marriage should encompass. Marriage is designed to be a reflection of your relationship with Christ.

Your marriage should testify to the world the love that Christ has for the church. Christ and the church are one, and so are you in your marriages. When you love God, and truly want to do His will, you then realize that your marriage should testify to the way your relationship should be with the Lord. You also realize the importance of working through your marriage and making it be the reflection that God wants it to be. This is true even as individuals. You need to understand that God made you in his image.

Marriage was not intended to satisfy your own needs and desires. Marriage is much bigger than that. This is the reason that Satan attacks marriages. God intended for marriage partners to operate as one unit in order to bring forth spiritually, mentally and emotionally sound individuals. When Satan attacks marriages, he is trying to bring down the human race and separate them from God's plan. A marriage operating as designed testifies to God's

Do you believe that you have shown your spouse your true commitment? What are some things that you can do to demonstrate your commitment?

_____

_____

_____

_____

_____

_____

_____

_____

_____

_____

_____

_____

So God created mankind in his own image, in the image of God he created them; male and female he created them. God blessed them and said to them, "Be fruitful and increase in number; fill the earth and subdue it…"

Genesis 1:27—28, NIV

glory, and promotes God's plan for healthy families, who then also breed healthy future marriages.

Marriage should be operating as one flesh in order to succeed. Becoming "one flesh" is not just through getting married or having sex. This is a process. It doesn't happen overnight. It takes devotion, dedication, and prayer to achieve unity. Then it takes devotion, dedication, and prayer for each spouse to empower the other to live in this unity. It is important that we understand that we were not meant to be alone.

Adam saw that there was none suitable for him. The Hebrew word for suitable is "kenegdo," meaning "equal." God Himself saw that it was not good for man to be alone, and therefore made the woman as his equal. God did not intend for a woman to be seen as less than a man.

Together "ezer kenegdo," translated into "suitable helper," really translates into an equal rescuer, an equal strength, and equal help. Woman was not made inferior. Of course, God gave each of us a role. Yes, you are to respect your husband as the head of the household. However, this is not because you are inferior. On the contrary, every leader needs a strong helper, and every leader is unable to do all things on their own.

I believe that God's making Eve from Adam's rib is an example of how man and woman belong together as one. It was not good for man to be alone, there was no one suitable for him, and he was in need of a helper. However, woman was made from

The Lord God said, "It is not good for the man to be alone. I will make a helper suitable for him."

Now the Lord God had formed out of the ground all the wild animals and all the birds in the sky. He brought them to the man to see what he would name them; and whatever the man called each living creature, that was its name. So the man gave names to all the livestock, the birds in the sky and all the wild animals.

But for Adam no suitable helper was found. So the Lord God caused the man to fall into a deep sleep; and while he was sleeping, he took one of the man's ribs and then closed up the place with flesh.

Then the Lord God made a woman from the rib he had taken out of the man, and he brought her to the man.

The man said,

"This is now bone of my bones
and flesh of my flesh;
she shall be called 'woman,'
for she was taken out of man."

That is why a man leaves his father and mother and is united to his wife, and they become one flesh."

Genesis 2:18—23, NIV

man, to show her need for him as well. The fact that God chose to make woman from man, instead of forming woman from dust alone, shows His idea of what our relationship with one another should be. It demonstrates our need for one another in our marriages.

He made woman from the rib, which is a part of the body that is on the side, to show how comparable they should be. The rib is under Adam's arm to show the protection and love women are to receive from their husbands. Also, the rib is a bone that protects the most vital and important organs, demonstrating the important role wives have in protecting (ezer) their husbands as well.

Adam was enthusiastic when he saw Eve. Adam understood that Eve was a gift. He stated that she is "bone of his bone and flesh of his flesh," so he understood the significance, and how precious she was. He understood that because she came out of him, he was to receive her as his own flesh and join to her as one.

When a man and woman join their lives together, they both should acknowledge their need for one another. Both should acknowledge their spouse as a gift. The marriage will only be successful if *both* acknowledge this and give to each other the love, respect, and honor they each require. When one spouse fails to do this, it can be detrimental to the relationship.

Husbands - understand that your wife is good. Notice that Proverbs 18:22 (page 39) does not say, "He who finds a *good* wife;

What are some ways that you can show your spouse that you value them in your life?

_____

_____

_____

_____

_____

_____

_____

_____

_____

_____

_____

_____

_____

_____

_____

_____

He who finds a wife finds what is good and receives favor from the Lord.

Proverbs 18:22, NIV

it simply says "a wife." The wife that God has given you as a gift is good, and she is a gift from the Lord.

Wives - your husband is a gift to you as well. You were designed to be his helper, his companion, because it wasn't good for him to be alone. Remember that you were specially made. Therefore, a wife must honor God and His love for her husband and man must love and honor his wife.

In Summary

This plan, this blueprint, this design that God intended is not always easy to grasp. However, if you choose to follow God's plan instead of the world's pattern, you will find that it can be a great blessing for your marriage.

If you now know what God's blueprint and design is for your marriage, it is up to you individually to do all you can to allow His design and plan to be the ruler of your actions. You must follow all that He has in store for you. Not only will it be a blessing for you, but it will be a blessing for your spouse and your children. God is the Architect, has designed and made a blueprint, and you must choose to accept that blueprint and build your lives according to His design. There is much more to His plan and design.

We'll discover together in the following chapters how everything fits into His design. All the steps and pieces, just as you would find in a construction project. The design alone is simply

Describe how you can change to reflect God's plan for marriage in your life.

_____

_____

_____

_____

_____

_____

_____

_____

_____

_____

_____

_____

not enough to make something beautiful, there are steps and other workings that follow in order to make a design come to life. God supplies us with the design and all the tools we need in order to make our marriages become what He has planned for us.

It can be difficult, but it is possible. Not in our own strength, but with His strength. God loves His children and wants nothing but beauty in their lives. My marriage is far from perfect, but it is better today than it was yesterday, and will be better tomorrow than today. I may not know all the secrets and I am growing daily. But, one thing that I know with all my heart is that if I trust God, and obey His commands, that He will put everything in its place, and this includes my marriage, my children, my family, and my friends. His design, His blueprint is better than anything that I can design or plan for. Let's work on this project together, discovering all of the wonderful joys that the Lord has for us.

Chapter One - Discussion Questions

Prior to reading this chapter, what did you believe was the purpose of your marriage? If your belief changed, in what ways did it change?

_____

_____

_____

_____

_____

_____

_____

_____

_____

_____

_____

_____

_____

_____

_____

_____

_____

Chapter One – Take Action!

Compare your answer to the question on page 41, with that of your wife's answer on women's page 41. Plan the ways that you both will contribute to your marriage, so that you will live according to God's blueprint.

_____

_____

_____

_____

_____

_____

_____

_____

_____

_____

Chapter Two

FOUNDATION

Look! I am placing a foundation stone…
a precious cornerstone that is safe to build on…
Isaiah 28:16, NLT

O nce you receive the blueprints that were drawn and designed by the Architect for your marriage, then the actual work begins. This is a construction project and each step is important in the process. Each task should be completed without taking any shortcuts. Once Luis and I knew what God's design was, we each had to work hard to follow it.

With any project, after the plans are drawn, the first crucial step is the laying down of the foundation. If the foundation is not done correctly, everything in the rest of the project is compromised. A building project is built and sits on its foundation, just as your entire relationship will sit on the foundation you set for your marriage.

I found out very quickly that the most important part of my life and my marriage was my communication, relationship, and connection with God. Christ should be in the center of our lives and our marriages. All the truths that we have learned, and all that He has shown us through His grace and mercy, were only possible to recognize through communication with Him.

For Luis it is the same. That day when we both found ourselves at the church prayer meeting, ready to talk to God and pray for each other, was a breakthrough for us. Not only did it show me that my husband cared enough for our marriage, and for me, to go to God about it. It also showed me that it was the only way that I was going to be at my best. It showed me that it was the only way we were going to have success in our marriage.

I am such a perfectionist. I am always trying to plan properly. I am always trying to make sure that everything comes out right. I am very detailed oriented and look to make the best plans possible. It was difficult for me to relinquish my control because I liked being in control. I always thought I was right. We women may often struggle with this trait.

I had to learn to give it all to God to control. In order for me to do that, I had to start by acknowledging my need for God in my life and then try to follow Him the best way I could. I had to build a relationship with the Lord by continuously communicating with him. Luis had to do the same. However, as much as it is difficult

What are some things that you have to surrender to the Lord?

for me to admit, Luis had a better time in this area because he was more willing to give control to God.

We both had to build communication with the Lord. It is only through communication with Him, that we can hear from Him. *How can we obey someone we cannot hear? How can we know what to do if we cannot receive the instructions?* Our primary foundation is communication. First build communication with God, and then build communication with each other.

Communication With God

If you want to have a healthy, successful marriage, you first need to start with yourself. You cannot possibly be your best self without allowing God in your life to help you. In order to do this, you need to build a personal relationship with Him.

It's important to understand that God loves you. His love is the rebar in the concrete of your marriage's foundation, the structure that strengthens our relationship with God. The enemy tries to weaken your relationship with God by putting doubt in your mind concerning God's love for you.

God loves you. Christ came and died on the cross to redeem us all. He loved you first, and His love doesn't change, no matter what condition you are in. The enemy tells you the lie that you are no good, or not good enough for God's love. Many people hold themselves back from even trying to have a relationship with God

List several things you can do to build your communication
with God.

_____

_____

_____

_____

_____

_____

_____

_____

_____

_____

_____

*For this is how God loved the world: He gave his one and only
Son, so that everyone who believes in him will not perish but
have eternal life*

John 3:16, NLT

We love because he first loved us.

1 John 4:19, ESV

because they feel that they would never be good enough. One of the many sayings that I have heard is, "If I were to go to church, the church would collapse". Some are so hard on themselves that they deny themselves a new start, and deny themselves a wonderful life in the Lord. If that is you, do not let the enemy continue to lie to you in this way.

> *but God shows his love for us in that while we were still sinners, Christ died for us.*
>
> **Romans 5:8 ESV**

Christ chose to give His life for you even though you are a sinner. He loves you regardless of who you are and what you've done. Satan will try to convince you that you are beyond loving, and will try to make you feel guilty of your past. Satan will try to bring constant condemnation to your life. We have all messed up. We have all committed sin, and we all have failed the Lord.

But, God loves you so much that He sent His son to die for you, so that you might have new life in Him. He offers forgiveness through Christ and His sacrifice. You only have to accept His sacrifice and accept Christ into your heart.

God gives the right to become His child when you accept the sacrifice that Christ made. When you believe and ask for forgiveness, He gives righteousness in exchange for your sins. When you accept Christ in your life as your Savior, you are made

Compose an affirmation that describes how God loves you.

_____

_____

_____

_____

_____

_____

_____

_____

_____

_____

For everyone has sinned: we all fall short of God's glorious standard.

Romans 3:23, NLT

But to all who believed him and accepted him, he gave the right to become children of God.

John 1:12, NLT

Therefore, if anyone is in Christ, he is a new creation; old things have passed away; behold, all things have become new.

2 Corinthians 5:17, NKJV

brand new; you are a new creation. God offers you a new life. Be confident knowing that God will not only make you brand new, but He will forgive and forget all of your sins. His saving grace is a wonderful right that is a gift to you; you can't take credit for it. You just have to be willing to accept the gift, willing to turn off the lies that you hear about God's love and forgiveness.

If you have not accepted Christ as your Savior, or have not been living in relationship with Him, you can freely ask Christ into your heart, tell him that you accept His sacrifice on the cross, and now want to have a life with Him in it. It is that simple to begin. You are invited to create a relationship with him by intentionally getting to know God through prayer, worship and His Word.

Another reason Christ gave His life on the cross was so that your communication with Him would no longer be limited. In the Old Testament, only the High Priest was allowed to approach the dwelling place of God in the temple. The design of the temple included a large curtain to create a separation from the people, and even the High Priest was only allowed in this area once a year.

When Christ gave His life on the cross, this curtain in the temple was torn.

> *"At that moment the curtain of the temple was torn in two from top to bottom..."*
>
> **Matthew 27:51 NIV**

Think about what your prayer life looks like. Write down some things that may need changing.

For I will forgive their wickedness and will remember their sins no more.

Hebrews 8:12, NIV

God saved you by his grace when you believed. And you can't take credit for this; it is a gift from God

Ephesians 2:8, NLT

The significance of the torn curtain was that there was no longer a barrier between God and you. You can now go to our Lord freely in prayer and speak to Him. There is no need for someone to do this on your behalf. You have a direct line of communication to your Father in Heaven.

How wonderful that one of the first things that happened after Christ gave His life on the cross was that direct communication with God was encouraged. In my opinion, this shows how much God wanted a relationship with you, that the curtain was one of the first physical things that was discarded when Christ gave His life.

Once you've established communication with God, you're able to hear from Him, and learn to recognize his voice. It's important to obey what He says. Your life depends on this truth.

Everyone then who hears these words of mine and does them will be like a wise man who built his house on the rock. And the rain fell, and the floods came, and the winds blew and beat on that house, but it did not fall, because it had been founded on the rock. And everyone who hears these words of mine and does not do them will be like a foolish man who built his house on the sand. And the rain fell, and the floods came, and the winds blew and beat against that house, and it fell, and great was the fall of it.

Matthew 7:24-27 ESV

List some of the things that you know God is telling you to do in your relationship with Him.

My sheep listen to my voice; I know them, and they follow me.
John 10:27, NLT

These verses express the importance of building your life foundation on Christ. If you build your life on Christ, nothing can shake you in any area of your life, including your marriage.

However, if you don't, your personal life, and everything else, will demolish because the foundation was not built correctly. Your foundation in the Lord should be built through prayer and His Word. It is important that you do this to become the men and women God intended you to be. If you build your marriage on Christ, you are sure that nothing can break it.

It is important that both spouses take part in this foundation. A marriage has two people, and both need to do their best for the other. It is foolish to build your house on the sand, and not the rock. It is foolish to build your marriage on anything else that is not Christ, who is the Rock! It is foolish to hear from God, know His Word and not follow His instruction.

One of the important ways you communicate with God is through prayer. "Prayer," as defined in the dictionary[2], is "an address (as a petition) to God or a god in word or thought, or an earnest request or wish." It is so great that you have someone to present your requests to.

---

[2]*Merriam-Webster.com.* (2015). Retrieved September 7, 2016, from Merriam-Webster: http://www.merriam-webster.com/dictionary/prayer

Write a prayer for your marriage.

"do not be anxious about anything, but in everything by prayer and supplication with thanksgiving let your requests be made known to God."

Philippians 4:6 ESV

Prayer is simply speaking to God, and God allows you to bring your petitions to Him. He cares about what your needs and desires are because He loves you. You just have to be willing to talk to Him. Talk to Him at all times, and about everything.

God wants constant communication with you. The best thing about this is that you do not have to pretend to be anybody else; you can be yourself because God already knows you. Something awesome is that you don't need eloquent words. All you need to do is open up your mind, your heart, and speak to God. He is ready, willing and able to listen to you. You will never bother Him.

God knew you before you were even formed in the womb. You can express yourself freely without any fear, transparently, at any time and from any place. Be open and honest. This is the best way to have communication with God.

Communication does not only involve talking, it also involves listening. Just as you need to talk to God, you need to listen to Him. God will speak to you in different ways. However, the best way He'll speak to you is through His Word.

Write a personal petition to the Lord.

_____

_____

_____

_____

_____

_____

_____

_____

_____

_____

_____

_____

pray without ceasing; give thanks in all circumstances; for this is the will of God in Christ Jesus for you.

1 Thessalonians 5:17-18, ESV

Before I formed you in the womb I knew you.

Jeremiah 1:5, ESV

All Scripture is inspired by God and is useful to teach us what is true and to make us realize what is wrong in our lives. It corrects us when we are wrong and teaches us to do what is right.

2 Timothy 3:16 NLT

God gives you His Word to teach you, to help you, and to speak to you. Through the help of the Holy Spirit, you are able to understand what God has to say to you in His Word. When you pray and meditate on His Word, God reveals to you what He wants you to know. Your communication with Him is not one-sided; you speak to Him, and He speaks back. He listens to us, and you should listen back. Communication takes both individuals to work.

In order to make communication work, there has to be trust. You can absolutely trust God. He knows you better than you know yourself. He knows what is best for you. He loves you. He sacrificed Himself for you. The trust you should have in the Lord is greater than any other trust you can have. Trust, transparency, and devotion are very important to developing your relationship.

You will find that after you've started to build communication with the Lord, the communication you build with your spouse is a bit easier, too. This is mainly because both of you are trying to be better versions of yourselves out of obedience to God. By being better versions of yourselves, you are able to be better to each other. This does not mean that you'll be perfect, or won't make any

What are some things that you can honestly say that you have not entrusted God fully with? You have tried giving, but still hold on to?

_____

_____

_____

_____

_____

_____

_____

_____

_____

_____

_____

_____

Trust in the Lord with all your heart...

Proverbs 3:5, NKJV

Blessed is the man who trusts in the Lord, And whose hope is the Lord.

Jeremiah 17:7, NKJV

mistakes. All are imperfect; however, you are instructed by the Word to continue forward and to imitate Christ. Therefore, you are striving to be better versions of yourself by obeying the Lord.

Obeying the Lord helps you to treat one another with love. This was one of His greatest commandments. Jesus Himself declared which were the two most important commandments.

> *Teacher, which is the great commandment in the Law?" And he said to him, "You shall love the Lord your God with all your heart and with all your soul and with all your mind. This is the great and first commandment. And a second is like it: You shall love your neighbor as yourself. On these two commandments depend all the Law and the Prophets.*
>
> **Matthew 22:36-40 ESV**

When you begin to follow these two commands, you not only build communication with the Lord, but then you begin to build communication with each other. You should love each other as you love yourselves. In order to love each other as you love yourselves, you must know each other through communication.

Communication with Each Other

While the first part of the foundation is communication with God, communication with each other comes next. Better communication with each other will support and strengthen other areas of your marriage. These include better relationship, resolving conflict, sexual intimacy, decision-making and others. Sharing with each other is the first step to communication.

Just like when communicating with God, you must be transparent with each other. After the Lord, your spouse should be the person you are most transparent with. You both should feel free to share your feelings, concerns, joys, etc., with each other.

> *Now the man and his wife were both naked, but they felt no shame.*
> **Genesis 2:25 NLT**

There should be no shame, even in your most vulnerable moments. Both spouses should absolutely share with each other, but sharing requires trust. Married individuals, have such a special relationship with each other. Your spouse sees and knows you in an intimate way that others do not. To develop this vital trust, both partners must prove themselves worthy of trust by not being judgmental with each other, and by keeping private matters private.

With love, there is no fear; no fear means there is trust. You have to vigilantly protect your spouse's trust, in order to keep an open channel to freely communicate with each other. Free communication can be life changing, and marriage saving.

Because of the communication I share with my husband, I am able to understand him better. Through many years of marriage, I had to learn more about my husband, how he grew up, and the experiences he went through. Learning of how he grew up and his earlier experiences, helped me to be more understanding in times that I necessarily didn't agree with how he was acting, or handling things. Luis learning of mine did the same for him.

I previously stated that God knows you and understands you better than you know yourself, but it is not the same for your spouse. Your spouse needs to learn about you in order to understand you. This only comes through communication, through trust, and sharing freely. Your spouse cannot read your mind, or even pretend to know how you feel about something unless you share this with them first.

However, when you are sharing and expressing yourself, you should make sure that you don't offend your spouse. Consider your partner's feelings. Make sure you think about what you are sharing or saying. Make sure the timing is right.

> *Everyone enjoys a fitting reply; it is wonderful to say the right thing at the right time!*
> **Proverbs 15:23 NLT**

Another important thing to keep in mind is that sometimes there are feelings that do not need to be expressed. Don't misunderstand what I'm saying. You should be open and free with

Have you shown your spouse that you can be trusted? What are some ways you can show your spouse that you are there for them, and that they can trust you?

_____

_____

_____

_____

_____

_____

_____

_____

_____

_____

_____

_____

_____

There is no fear in love. But perfect love drives out fear, because fear has to do with punishment. The one who fears is not made perfect in love."

1 John 4:18, NIV

one another. Sometimes your spouse may not be ready to receive something you want to share. Sometimes it may do more harm than good. You need to use prudence with what you are sharing.

> *When words are many, transgression is not lacking, but whoever restrains his lips is prudent.*
> **Proverbs 10:19, ESV**

The one you need to be the most free with is the Lord. The Lord is always willing to listen; some things just need to be taken to Him. Timing in what to say, and when to say it, can mean a difference between understanding and misunderstanding.

The art of expression and exchanging of information, ideas, thoughts and feelings is one of the key things when it comes to communication. However, in order for the expression and exchanging of information to be effective, the other party has to be listening.

You have to listen to each other. It is good to share, but one person doing all the sharing is not good enough, and one person doing all the listening is not good enough either.

Sometimes one person in the marriage can be the one who always likes to talk. While it is good to be a person who likes to share all the time, the person always talking can sometimes overpower the other person's ability to also share. This can even cause poor communication lines to shut down completely.

Are you sharing with your spouse? Have been mindful of their feelings? Self-evaluate how you share with your spouse.

_____

_____

_____

_____

_____

_____

_____

_____

_____

_____

_____

_____

_____

_____

_____

_____

_____

For everything there is a season, and a time for every matter under heaven:

Ecclesiastes 3:1, ESV

...A time to keep silence, and a time to speak;

Ecclesiastes 3:7 ESV

The ability to listen can help to strengthen communication in marriage. The Word of God tells you that you should be quick to hear and slow to speak. You need to make sure that one person is not doing all the talking. Both have to listen to each other speak, meaning the person who is not the talkative one will have to give the other person the opportunity to listen to you speak.

Listening involves more than just being quiet. Listening involves being engaged with what the other is saying.

> *...listen to me, and be attentive to the words of my mouth.*
>
> **Proverbs 7:24 ESV**

There has to be a genuine interest of what the other person is saying. You must listen to all that person has to say and not only focus on what may interest you, or what offends or upsets you. That is called selective listening. Selective listening can damage the communication lines.

A good listener will make the other person feel that his or her voice or concerns are important. There also has to be respect of their point of view or interest. You may not agree, but you can still learn to respect their view.

Active listening increases your understanding for each other, which helps to build stronger communication. The adjective definition of the word "understanding," is to be sympathetically

Are you listening to your spouse? Have you been mindful of what they may want to share? Self-evaluate how you listen to your spouse.

You must be quick to listen, slow to speak...

James 1:19, NLT

aware of other people's feelings; tolerant and forgiving. Understanding involves compassion. Sometimes it may be difficult for you to understand your spouse. Especially when you might not agree with something that he or she is expressing.

Although this can be difficult, it is possible to overcome. You have to be intentional on listening with understanding. If you do not understand something, ask questions. The best sign of listening is asking specific questions on what that person is sharing. Ask questions that clarify what your spouse is saying. For example, if your spouse said, "I saw the car", and you want more information, you can ask, "What color was the car you saw?" I know this is a simple example, but if you notice, the question was specific about the car that was mentioned. This can help you to understand more completely what your spouse is sharing. It can help your spouse feel as though you are engaged and care about what they are sharing. This can be beneficial for both spouses.

However, some questions can cause contention. It is beneficial to listen with a positive attitude. If the speaker doesn't carefully choose their words, they could offend unintentionally. If this happens, first assume that they have good intentions, and ask for clarification before jumping to any wrong conclusions.

Luis and I have completely different styles of communicating. I naturally like to talk and like to teach. Since I was a child, I've felt compelled to help those in class struggling with schoolwork. I was a good student, but every year the teachers would write in the comment section of my report card, "Angela is a great student, but she talks too much, she must remember that she is not the teacher." Talking and trying to teach others is part of my personality. As a child, a teenager, and a mother it was fine. But, as a wife, this can be damaging.

There were times that Luis and I were discussing certain issues or topics, and if I thought Luis didn't understand my view, I would ask, "Do you know what the word so and so means". This would stir up an argument. Where I was trying to help him to understand what I was saying, he took my question as though I was actually talking down to him, as though he could not understand the words I was using.

Several things were wrong here. First, I did this sort of thing many times, and many times, I got the same type of response. The number one thing I had to learn was that although I did not mean harm in what I was saying, I was offending him. After the first argument that we had when I used this type of method, I should have tried another approach.

Luis also needed to learn to listen positively. Instead of receiving my question negatively and assuming that I was talking down to him, if he had a positive attitude and chose to believe that I would not intentionally offend him, he would have realized that I was just trying to explain what I meant.

Because he was taking his time to answer, and because he was asking certain questions, I would assume he did not understand. If

I expected a certain reaction or response, I would get frustrated that he did not understand me, and then proceed into teaching mode. I needed to be positive as well, and have patience. I had to wait and receive his full response before I decided that he did not understand me.

The most important lesson in this example is that Luis and I have two different styles of expression. We express ourselves differently and both of us needed to learn one another's style of expression. Just to summarize some of our styles of expression, I am open, talkative and like to be helpful and to respond quickly. Luis is more to himself, a man with not so many words. He only likes to respond if needed, and only when he has full information of the entire situation.

Learning each other's style was not an overnight process. This takes years and dedication to one another. It also takes desire. You will not learn about your spouse unless you desire to do so. Desire leads to effort, effort leads to understanding.

By wisdom a house is built,
and by understanding it is established.
Proverbs 24:3, ESV

We both had to learn not to think or act with our emotions. You cannot go based on your feelings all the time. Your feelings can get you into trouble. Depending on your emotional state for

What are some of the things you can work on when you communicate with your spouse?

the day, you can perceive things that may not necessarily be correct. Our emotions can be deceptive. Try to focus on what your spouse is trying to communicate, and not necessarily how it may be said or how you believe it came across.

If you are the communicator, try to break bad communication habits. Communicate clearly, do not leave things open for interpretation. Watch your tone of voice, your facial expressions, body language, or hand movements. Sometimes the listener is doing everything possible to be engaging and non-judgmental but your communication skills may need some adjusting.

When you communicate with your spouse, speak and listen respectfully, honestly and with love. Have a forgiving heart so that if they do say something that offends, you can respond with love instead of anger or hurt. Or if they are not giving you the attention you would like, you can talk to them about it. Remember not everyone thinks alike, and *the way the other person is processing your communication* may be the real issue, not your spouse.

> *Put on then, as God's chosen ones, holy and beloved, compassionate hearts, kindness, humility, meekness, and patience, bearing with one another and, if one has a complaint against another, forgiving each other; as the Lord has forgiven you, so you also must forgive. And above all these put on love, which binds everything together in perfect harmony.*
> **Colossians 3:12-14, ESV**

It is important that your communication is developed so that you could both learn each other's communicating styles, learn each other's likes and dislikes, learn the real intentions behind certain types of expressions, and so much more. Again, this is a process. You do not simply master communication because suddenly you are sharing well or listening well. It is a complete package and it is very possible to find the needed balance.

This does not mean that there will never be any type of misunderstandings going forward. Most certainly this can mean that you can now have the tools and knowledge to sort through the misunderstandings more efficiently, effectively, and above all more lovingly.

Another area that can be difficult is if you need to exercise correction with your spouse. You must learn that just because something is uncomfortable for you to hear, doesn't mean that you shouldn't hear it. Alternatively, just because something is uncomfortable to say, doesn't mean you shouldn't say it.

>*Therefore encourage one another*
>*and build each other up...*
>**1 Thessalonians 5:11 NIV**

Your spouse is supposed to help build you up. That may mean that they may have wisdom on what you are doing or saying. As long as it is done with love and with the affirmation from the Lord, that is what they are to do. Remember that the Lord may be using your spouse to communicate something life changing and important for your life.

If you give correction, then you must also be able to receive correction. Luis has often shown me areas of my life where I could be better, and vice versa. The key is that you are not looking to change your spouse. You are simply offering some insight on an area you see that may be a struggle for them. Because I am naturally always trying to be the helpful one, the one who teaches, this area was difficult for me. I had to learn not to be so correcting all the time, but I also had to learn to be able to receive correction. This should all be done in love, and again with the affirmation of the Lord. If not, it can backfire and cause contention.

Remember it is not your job to change your spouse. That is the job of the Holy Spirit. While the Holy Spirit can prompt you to speak into the life of your spouse, you have to make sure that the prompting is from the Holy Spirit and not your own hidden agenda. Bear in mind that you must also be willing to receive loving correction from your spouse, because it might be the Lord speaking to you through them.

You can take these steps when looking to *give* correction to your spouse:

- *Pray* - Make sure that the correction you are about to give your spouse is indeed from the Lord. If it is not, it can backfire. Make sure your intentions are not selfish; pray to God to search your heart. (Psalms 139:23)

Do you receive correction well from your spouse? If not, what are ways you can change?

_____

_____

_____

_____

_____

_____

_____

_____

_____

_____

So a church leader must be a man whose life is above reproach…he must be able to teach.

1 Timothy 3:2, NLT

When she (wife) speaks, her words are wise, and she gives instruction with kindness.

Proverbs 31:26, NLT

- *Timing* - Make sure that the timing is right; their acceptance to what you want to share can ultimately depend on when you communicate it. (Ecclesiastes 3:7)
- *Choose* - Make sure that you choose the right words to express yourself. The timing may be right, and your intentions good, but the wrong words can cause conflict. (Ephesians 4:29)
- *Truth* - The main reason you are taking this step is because you love them. Make sure you're honest and loving as you speak truth into their lives. (Ephesians 4:15)

You can take these steps when you *receive* correction from your spouse:

- *Listen* - Take the time to hear your spouse out. Do not be on the defensive. (Proverbs 19:20)
- *Pray* - Pray about what your spouse has shared and get confirmation from the Lord as to how to apply it to your life. (Psalms 139:24)
- *Choose* - Choose to accept the correction graciously. It can lead to gaining wisdom, (Proverbs 15:32, Proverbs 8:33)
- *Thank* - Thank the Lord and then your spouse for their love, and make sure that you acknowledge how they have helped you. There is no shame in this. (Psalms 28:7)

Do you give correction well to your spouse? What are ways you can change?

But the fruit of the Spirit is love, joy, peace, patience, kindness, goodness, faithfulness, gentleness, self-control: against such things there is no law.

Galatians 5:22-23, ESV

If you are practicing your communication with God, when the time comes that the Lord is using your spouse, you will have the ability to detect it. Maybe not right away, but after careful analysis and prayer you will be able to acknowledge that the Lord was using your spouse to help you.

If it should take time and not be something that you notice immediately, make sure to communicate to your spouse your gratitude for the courage it took for them to lovingly show you something you could not see yourself. Communicating this can be encouraging to your spouse, and they would take their role in this part of communication more seriously, to ensure that it is not abused.

In Summary

Communication is an important part of any relationship. Communication with God can help you to be better in so many ways. You can be a better person because God will be communicating ways that you can be better for yourself, your family, your friends, and especially your spouse. As you communicate with God through prayer, worship, and through the Bible, you will grow spiritually and the fruit of the Spirit will manifest itself in you, helping you to treat each other better.

You should be actively exercising communication both with God and with your spouse. Communication is an important foundation that can make all other areas of your marriage better including relationship, resolving conflict, sexual intimacy, decision-making and others areas. Your marriage cannot afford lack of communication. Try every effort to lay this foundation right and not compromise the rest of the structure.

Chapter Two - Discussion Questions

What are some of the ways your wife communicates with you? What can you do to react more positively when your communication style differs from hers?

_____

_____

_____

_____

_____

_____

_____

_____

_____

_____

_____

_____

_____

_____

Chapter Two – Take Action!

Compare your answer to the question on page 73, with that of your wife's answer on women's page 73. Identify the ways that you both will initiate and build on your communication skills, to create a stronger foundation for your marriage.

Chapter Three

SPECIALIST

I praise you, for I am fearfully and wonderfully made...
Psalm 139:14, ESV

S o far, the blueprints are drawn and the foundation laid, and now the real work begins. Each of you has a role and responsibility in the project. In any construction project, it's important that everyone does their particular job or function in order for the project to be a success. You're charged with your particular task and no one can do that task other than you. If you're a specialist within a project, no one can do it better than you can.

Everyone else's effort to do your specialty will fall short and the construction project will suffer if you, the best person for the job, aren't on task. You have a very special purpose in your relationship. Your wife can't do what you are tasked by God to do and you as a husband and/or father are not able to do what your wife is tasked by God to do. In this construction project, God is the designer and owner of the project, and you are to follow His orders.

As a man, a husband, and a father, I fully understand how difficult it can be to feel that you are doing a good job in all these areas. We can be so hard on ourselves and want to be the best husband for our wife, our family, and ourselves. But you can't give up! God can give you exactly what you need. You can't allow doubt to enter your mind.

A double minded man is unstable in all his ways.
James 1:8, NLT

I had to learn this, and many other things, in order to be who God called me to be. Being double minded will only lead down a path of destruction and instability. You can't allow negative thoughts to enter your heart or your mind. Negative thoughts can lead you to believe wrongful things about yourself and or your wife. Some of these thoughts can prompt you to think that you are not a good husband, or that you are unable to do things correctly. When you are unstable in your thinking, you do not allow yourself to be the man you are meant to be.

As men, we are affected by our egos. When others hurt your ego, it can be harmful, but when you allow your own thinking to hurt your ego, it can be even more harmful. It can be easier for us to dismiss what others have to say, but when we get it into our heads that something about ourselves is true, it can be harder for us to be able to release or let go of that misconception or lie.

Your thoughts have to be firm and concentrated on what God has to say about every situation. The enemy attacks your thoughts in order to provoke all types of negative responses in every area of your life. In other words, if the enemy can attack what you think about yourself, then he can affect how you respond, with your words, and with your actions. The only way to be strong against the enemy when these attacks come is to ensure your relationship with the Lord is strong. This was one of the first things I had to start putting into action when I decided that I wanted to be a better man, a better husband, and a better father.

Man to Man

Man to man, I want to talk to you about how and what I had to do for my marriage, my family, and myself. It wasn't easy. In the first two chapters, we went over with you the importance of knowing God's design and plan for our marriages. We went over communication and how important it is to communicate with God and your wife. My wife and I went through some difficult times, and I know that if God wasn't in our lives, we would not be where we are today.

We don't have a perfect marriage. We still have our ups and downs, but now we are better at working things out. Although we have been married for over 20 years, I am still learning how to be a better husband and father, and a better man. I've learned that with God's help I can absolutely become the man, the husband, and the father He created me to be.

We as men sometimes get caught up with what we think should happen. We like things to go a certain way, and when it doesn't work in that way, we get frustrated, disappointed, and discouraged. This led me to act out, or take out my frustrations on my wife, and my children. I saw that my marriage wasn't going well, and because of the love I had for my wife and my children, I realized I had to make a change.

God First

First thing I had to do was to put my priorities in order. In the beginning of my relationship with my wife, I did so many things for her out of love. She was my main focus. As the troubles came, my focus began to shift from her to myself. Because I felt she was not holding up to my standards, I began not to do for her as much. I allowed my disappointment to dictate what I would and wouldn't do for her. This was all wrong, and because my priorities weren't in the correct order, I allowed other things to distract me from being the husband God wanted me to be. As I was putting my wife as my number one priority, when she let me down, it was easy for me to shift away from taking care of her the way I needed to. I was putting too many expectations on my wife, when in fact my number one priority should've been God.

You need to make your relationship with the Lord your number one priority. The Lord, and the Lord alone, should be number one. Don't confuse God with the church. The church is not first, God is first. We are to do our part in the church and plug in where the Lord wills, but the church is not God. You make God your number one priority by seeking God through prayer, His word, praise and fasting. You need to put in practice the communication we spoke to you about in chapter 2.

When you put God first, He will make sure to provide all the other things that you need in your life. He begins to put in order all that is out of order. He will help you to realize and accept the things that are in your heart that need to change. Men, you need to love more. Love your God more, and love your wife more. Out of love, is why you sacrifice. Out of love, is how you find redemption. The Lord will give you the prime example of how to love sacrificially. Not only does He provide this example, but He provides what is necessary to lead.

Many men want to be a leader in some way. It can be very rewarding to be appreciated and acknowledged as the leader. But, appreciation and acknowledgement should not be the main reasons that you lead. You should lead because you want to ensure things

Is God your number 1 priority? What changes do you need to make to enrich your relationship with the Lord?

_____

_____

_____

_____

_____

_____

_____

_____

_____

_____

_____

Seek the Kingdom of God above all else, and live righteously, and he will give you everything you need.

Matthew 6:33, NLT

And it is my prayer that your love may abound more and more, with knowledge and all discernment.

Philippians 1:9, ESV

are done right. You should lead because you want to work for the best possible outcome in every situation.

I learned to be the true leader through my relationship with God. God provides wisdom and discernment, as you need it. Through His wisdom and discernment, you are able to make the right decisions, and are able to know what is best for your relationship with your wife. This is not easy. It's not like when we talk to a friend and we always have an instant response. God does provide all the answers we need in His Word, in His own time.

It is vitally important, for yourself and for your marriage, that you seek the Lord in prayer. As a man and leader, you should pray daily. I can't stress enough how important this is. It is one of the main ways you put your relationship with God first. Just as you need to cultivate your relationship with your wife, you need to do so with the Lord. This is the only way that you will learn to be the man and leader God has called you to be. Take advantage of the blessing God gives, that you don't have to do things on your own. Accept the Lord's help in every area of your life. The Lord is more than willing, and more than able, to provide you with the wisdom and discernment you need to be the leader he has called.

God wants you to lead as a wise, discerning and experienced man. But, you must be willing to make changes in order to be the man He wants you to be. Through increased relationship with Him, you will gain the character you need. I can tell you from experience that the things I placed in the hands of the Lord were

Write down areas that are a struggle, in which you would like the Lord's help to gain wisdom and discernment.

_____

_____

_____

_____

_____

_____

_____

_____

_____

_____

_____

If you need wisdom, ask our generous God, and he will give it to you. He will not rebuke you for asking.

James 1:5, NLT

Choose for yourselves wise and discerning men, known to your tribes, and appoint them as your leaders.

Deuteronomy 1:13, ISV

the very things that came out best. The Lord guided me and helped me to deal with even the situations that seemed impossible. One of the things I can stress to you is that your impossibilities are not impossible for God. So if you feel as though the things you are dealing with are impossible to resolve, reject that thought. Choose instead to believe in the Lord Almighty.

All your responsibilities can seem overwhelming at times, but know that you do not have to do anything alone. Know that God has equipped you with the best tools available. You have to place your trust in Him, and allow the Lord to fill you with all the wisdom and discernment He has to offer. You may not know it yet, but He has already begun to do this very thing. He made you specifically to be a leader, and has already placed in you the desire and the ability to lead. But, it's not complete without Him.

God continuously challenges you to be better because He knows you can be, because you're made in His image. Throughout the Word of God, we see how God not only states that He made man in His image, but then He goes on to compare who we should be with His perfect Son, Jesus. God has made you in such a great way, that He states how you are to be Christ-like. If He says that you can be Christ-like through the power and help of the Holy Spirit it is because you can be, and in your marriage, it is the same.

God tells you to love your wife as Christ loved the church. It's a tall order to love your wives as Christ loved the church. To do this, you have to allow God to make some changes in you first, to make you into that wise, experienced, and discerning man. I had to learn that I was imperfect and that I had to allow God to change in me the things that needed to be changed.

Called to Lead

God began to reveal this truth to me through prayer and fasting. For a long time, I wanted my wife to change, but God helped me realize that I needed to change. For so long, I blamed her for all the things I thought she was doing wrong, and I never looked at myself. God showed this to me. He showed me that I was not being the leader He called me to be.

As I was praying, I was complaining to God about my marriage and my wife. I complained about all she was doing to me, and all she wasn't doing for me. I complained about how she was not being the wife I expected her to be. Then God led me to Ephesians 5:23 (page 95), when I saw "Savior of his body", I realized that I was not acting like a Savior when I complained. She was part of me, and I was coming against her, so in reality I was coming against myself, and a Savior doesn't come against anyone. A Savior sacrifices for the sake of simply saving.

God has called the man to be the leader of his home, but you must know exactly what this means. You see the words, "head of his wife" and automatically may assume that it means that you are suppose to rule over her. You might think that your wife should simply obey, but leadership is not about being a dictator. A true leader motivates, inspires and guides. I was dictating to my wife, and I wasn't motivating, inspiring, or guiding her. A leader communicates with transparency. I needed to communicate in a better way to my wife as I led her.

Wives Next

When you see the words "head of his wife", don't miss the rest of the passage, "as Christ is the head of the church". This is an important analogy. Christ doesn't dictate to you, or simply rule over you. Christ will motivate, inspire, and guide you. The verse goes on to say that, "He is the Savior of his body, the church". Christ is your Savior, and like him, you must do everything in your power to protect your wife. After God, your most important priority is your wife, then your children. Yes, your children are a priority but the order is God, wife, and then children. The Bible is clear on that order.

> *31"Therefore a man shall leave his father and mother and hold fast to his wife, and the two shall become one flesh." 32 This mystery is profound, and I am saying that it refers to Christ and the church. 33 However, let each one of you love his wife as himself, and let the wife see that she respects her husband.*
>
> **Ephesians 5:31-33**

Have you demonstrated to your wife that she is a main priority in your life? What ways can you show her?

_____

_____

_____

_____

_____

_____

_____

_____

_____

_____

_____

_____

For a husband is the head of his wife as Christ is the head of the church. He is the Savior of his body, the church.

Ephesians 5:23, NLT

In chapter one, we have already talked about joining with your spouse as one flesh as a reason to show why you were meant to be married, but there is more to it than that. Verse 31 explains not only the joining of two individuals; it also expresses how you left your parents to be together.

You both are now responsible for each other in a way that is described as profound, and the verse compares it to Christ and the church. Just as the church is such a priority for Christ that he gave up His life for the church, your wife, after God, should be number one to you.

Raising children is a great responsibility, and should be the next priority. However, the job of raising your children only lasts a short time. The time will come that they will leave to start their own lives. When this happens, you and your wife are the last ones standing in your home. If you spent your years dedicating your time and effort to your children as your first priority, then when it's only the two of you, your relationship will have a void.

The emphasis that God puts on staying in marriage is an important one. Loving your wife the way Christ loved the church is also for the benefit of your children because she can be a better mother, nurturer, and friend to them if she is cared for the way God intended.

How should you treat your wife? What kind of relationship should you have with her? This is where it gets confusing. When you feel as though you aren't a priority, or if you're having some troubles, it's very hard for you to be motivated to be the loving husband that your wife expects. So I will share some of the things I did, that changed my marriage in a great way.

Needed Changes

I absolutely needed to change. As a man, this was hard for me to accept. One thing I had to learn was to let go of my pride. Pride tells you that you have nothing to change. Or, that you have always operated this way and you've been all right up to this point. Pride led me to become arrogant. Pride and arrogance are dangerous. I allowed pride and arrogance to control me. It deceived me.

It dominated my thinking, and the decisions that I was making. This led to many arguments and disagreements. You can't allow yourself to let pride dominate your thoughts or actions.

When this happens, not only will you act foolishly, but also you may make things a lot worse. You may do and say things that can cause great harm to your wife, your family and yourself. As leaders, we have to have a clear mind. We always have to think things thoroughly without any type of emotional influences. Not that you don't have the right to feel or have feelings about things, but those feelings shouldn't be what are driving your decisions.

Pride and arrogance are two feelings in particular that can be damaging in your life and in your heart. In a way, I allowed pride and arrogance to harden my heart, and when this happens, there can be many irreversible consequences. I let pride get in the way, and it almost destroyed my marriage. Things got so bad, I had made up my mind that no matter what my wife said, I was not going to listen or care. There were times I thought about giving up on my wife. I believed that my marriage was a wreck. I believed that there was no hope. I decided that I didn't want to stay married any longer. I decided that I wanted out.

Another area I struggled with was anger. There were many times that my wife and I got into very bad arguments. I allowed the arguments to grow into anger and resentment in my heart towards her. The enemy had me believing that the love that I had for her was diminishing. It was so bad that I couldn't see past my anger. I began asking myself, *is she ever going to change? Is it worth it for me to continue to be in this relationship? Am I the problem?*

I started asking myself questions. After a while, I had the attitude that if she wanted this marriage to work, then she was going to have to change her ways and give me the respect that I deserved. I had so much anger inside of me. I became self-centered. I didn't care about her thoughts or about how hurt she felt. I was acting very selfish.

After some time, I came to the realization that I was the one putting my marriage in jeopardy. My conduct towards my wife wasn't only affecting her and me. It was also affecting our kids. I thought about the void I felt because my father wasn't part of my

Have you let pride affect how you act toward your wife? Are there things that you can think of that you can begin to change?

_____

_____

_____

_____

_____

_____

_____

_____

_____

_____

But, when his heart became arrogant and hardened with pride, he was deposed from his royal throne and stripped of his glory.
Daniel 5:20, NIV

The pride of your heart has deceived you...
Obadiah 1:3, NIV

life. I remembered the struggles my mother had as a woman and as a single mother with four children. In no way did I want that for my wife or my kids.

I was angry with her, but deep down I loved her. Something had to give; I had to give in. I realized that I did, in fact, love my wife. So, I made the determination of not giving up on my wife or my kids because of the love that I had for them. I didn't want to be the man that abandoned his wife, like my father did to my mother, and I did not want my kids to grow up without their father being part of their everyday lives, just like my siblings and I had.

Take Responsibility

I started to seek God in prayer about my marriage. I struggled because I didn't want to let go of my pride or anger. I had to decide to let go of my pride and let God into every area of my life. I then had to surrender to the Lord, and ask Him to help me save my marriage.

I began to pray and fast for my marriage, for my kids. I realized that I was putting all the responsibility of my marriage on my wife. I realized that my attitude was not fair. I realized that I was blaming her for everything that went wrong. This is something that is a natural thing to do. When Adam and Eve sinned, blame shifting was their first response.

Have you let anger cloud your judgment? What are areas that you may need to exercise more love, care and patience with your wife?

_____

_____

_____

_____

_____

_____

_____

_____

_____

_____

Pride leads to conflict…

Proverbs 13:10, NLT

Pride goes before destruction…

Proverbs 16:18, NLT

When things go wrong, it is easier for us to pass the blame, instead of looking at our own fault in the situation. Yes, Eve gave the fruit to Adam, but Adam was his own man. He was responsible for his own actions. He should have taken charge of the situation and saved himself and his wife. It is the same for men now.

Men, you must take the responsibility to work hard for your marriage. You must fight for your wife. She is your responsibility to care for and to love, not to hate or mistreat. I say mistreat because anytime I was not giving her the love and respect that God had ordered me to do, I was, in fact, mistreating her.

One of the first ways that I asked God to help me was to give me a new heart. To change my ways, convict me, and reveal the mistakes I had made as a husband. I came to the realization that I had to allow God to do the work that only He knew how to do. I was constantly trying to fix things myself and take things into my own hands. But, God is the master at fixing things and making things right.

God will finish the work He started in you if you let Him. He will help you become the man you need to be. I had to allow God to enter into my areas of struggle and not allow the things that were doing harm to me to continue to rule me, or be a distraction to me. I didn't want for that anger, resentment, and pride to be part of me any longer. I had to surrender my life to God and let go of my pride, my anger, and my resentment.

Have you passed the blame on your wife? Are there areas that you can honestly look at that require you to examine yourself?

_____

_____

_____

_____

_____

_____

_____

_____

_____

_____

_____

The man replied, "It was the woman you gave me who gave me the fruit, and I ate it."

Genesis 3:12, NLT

You need to learn let go of pride. If not, it will govern you and bring destruction into your marriage. You must let go, and seek God. You have to humble yourself so that God can give you grace and show you favor.

You need to ask God to cut out any pride that you have in your heart. This is so that you will be able to move forward. If you don't surrender yourself before him and ask him to help you with this, it will tear your marriage apart.

You also need to let go of anger and resentment. Anger can lead to sin if you don't control it. Not that it is a sin to be angry. You are allowed to feel anger, but you are not allowed to let anger drive you to sin. For men, sometimes this can be difficult because men sometimes may not be as expressive with words as women are. Women tend to talk out their feelings and to discuss what they are going through. They tend to express what is bothering them.

Men tend to keep things bottled up. This causes for unresolved feelings of to grow, which can be a cause for anger to build. When anger builds and it is not dealt with in a healthy manner, anger can affect your actions. Then your actions, if you're not careful, can become sinful or harmful to yourself. In my marriage, when things weren't going as I wanted or planned, or when I felt that my wife was not doing her part or her "duty", I acted in ways that I never should have.

God provides help and grace for our shortcomings. List the areas you would like for God to begin working in you.

_____

_____

_____

_____

_____

_____

_____

_____

And I am certain that God, who began the good work within you, will continue his work until it is finally finished on the day when Christ Jesus returns.

Philippians 1:6, NLT

In your anger, do not sin: Do not let the sun go down while you are still angry,

Ephesians 4:26, NLT

But he gives us more grace. That is why Scripture says:
   "God opposes the proud
   but shows favor to the humble

James 4:6, NIV

The Leader He Called

There was a time that I felt that my wife was not submitting and respecting me the way she was supposed to. I was so busy being angry and resentful that I was blinded. I didn't see how I was contributing to what was happening in my marriage. I didn't see that the problem wasn't whether she failed to submit and respect me, as much as it was me failing to love her the way I should have loved her. I needed to love her with that motivational, inspiring love like Christ. In order for me to understand this, I had to search my heart, and turn to God's Word. I had to look at and understand all that God had to say.

Look at the passage in Ephesians 5:21-33 (page 107). Note that verse 21 tells us to submit to one another. We are to submit in different capacities, but we are to submit to one another out of reverence to God. My wife is to submit to me as a leader, but I am to submit to her as a lover and protector. I can't fail to submit to her as a lover and protector, because it is my love and protection that prompts her respect for me. In verse 31, we can see this very clearly. It lists the loving of your wife first, and then the wife respecting the husband. Your actions towards your wife are always first and will determine whether they inspire and motivate her, or whether they discourage and demotivate her.

21 And further, submit to one another out of reverence for Christ. 22 For wives, this means submit to your husbands as to the Lord. 23 For a husband is the head of his wife as Christ is the head of the church. He is the Savior of his body, the church. 24 As the church submits to Christ, so you wives should submit to your husbands in everything. 25 For husbands, this means love your wives, just as Christ loved the church. He gave up his life for her 26 to make her holy and clean, washed by the cleansing of God's word. 27 He did this to present her to himself as a glorious church without a spot or wrinkle or any other blemish. Instead, she will be holy and without fault. 28 In the same way, husbands ought to love their wives as they love their own bodies. For a man who loves his wife actually shows love for himself. 29 No one hates his own body but feeds and cares for it, just as Christ cares for the church. 30 And we are members of his body. 31 As the Scriptures say, "A man leaves his father and mother and is joined to his wife, and the two are united into one." 32 This is a great mystery, but it is an illustration of the way Christ and the church are one. 33 So again I say, each man must love his wife as he loves himself, and the wife must respect her husband.

Ephesians 5:21-33, NLT

Just because you are named leader of your home doesn't mean that God values you more. You're both one in Christ. In the eyes of the Lord there are no differences in your value, He loves you equally. However, there is a difference in the purpose you each serve and in how He has designed each of you. Nevertheless, each purpose is equally significant, and equally valuable. Therefore, you should value your wife and who she is in your life.

This union is so important that God saw it fit to compare it with Christ and the church. It is so great to know that God has us in such high regard that he would even make that type of analogy. Then He calls us His people. God loves every person and has a purpose for each one, but you and every person must choose His plan. For the husband it is to lead his wife, while loving and respecting her, for the wife it is to submit and respect her husband.

As men, we can also misunderstand what the word submission is. Submission does not mean that your wife is less valuable than you are. Submission doesn't mean that your wife doesn't have a say, or an identity. You should consider her input. Value her opinion, but make sure to pray and make the final decision according to how the Lord wills it in your heart.

This doesn't mean that you can't decide to go with what she suggests. Remember, she is your helper and as such, God may reveal something to her about the decision you should make. My wife is good with numbers and other things that I really don't have interest or the knowledge of. As a leader, I am wise enough to know that I can trust her with those responsibilities and tasks. When I need her to take over, I am wise enough to let her.

Submission doesn't mean that you are allowed to harm or mistreat your wife in any way. In verses 28-29 from Ephesians 5 (page 107), the Word states that when you love your wife you are actually showing love for yourself. This is so because your wife is one with you. She is part of you, and when you mistreat her, you are actually mistreating yourself. When you mistreat her, you are not caring for your own body. You are also not allowed to guide her into sin or any wrongdoing. You are to enrich her life, just as you would enrich your body with nourishment. Make sure that you are caring for and protecting your wife.

You are called to be her leader, but as Christ leads us into only what is good, so are you to lead your wife into what is good. Your wife is to submit to you as the church submits to Christ, but one very important thing is that Christ loved the church first. He sacrificed Himself first. He gave His life first. He served the church first. If you expect your wife to submit to you, as the church submits to Christ, you have to love her first, and you have to sacrifice yourself first. You have to serve her first, the way Christ did.

Love like Christ

How did I expect my wife to submit, love, and respect me if I was not doing everything that God wanted me to do for her first? In other words, Christ made the sacrifice to surrender His life, so that we can have life, because He loves us. Just as He sacrificed life for His the church, who represents his bride, I had to do the same for my bride.

If I wanted my marriage to last, I had to love and serve her as Christ loves and serves the Church. I had to make sacrifices to be more loving, patient, caring, and understanding. Because of the love Christ had for the church, he gave up His life for her. I had to be willing to sacrifice my entire life for my wife. I was definitely not doing that. Instead, I was blaming her, not loving her the way she needed to be loved, and more certainly not being Christ-like in any form.

If I wanted to show her that I loved her, I had to give up all the things that were causing strife in our marriage. Christ knew that the church didn't deserve this sacrifice, but He was willing to love her unconditionally anyway. He was willing to sacrifice His life anyway. I had to sacrifice in the same way. Even if I felt she didn't deserve my sacrifice, or even if I thought that she was not doing her part, I had to do it anyway.

A leader takes responsibility for the team. Christ gave up His life to make the church holy and clean, to present her as blameless and without fault. I spent so much time blaming my wife for the problems in our marriage, that I failed to understand that it was my responsibility to take the first steps to make it right. Christ took on all the blame for the sake of the church, so I had to accept full responsibility and move to cleaning up our marriage. I had to begin

What are your thoughts on submission? Is this an area you may have misunderstood?

_____

_____

_____

_____

_____

_____

_____

_____

_____

_____

_____

_____

There is no longer Jew or Gentile, slave or free, male or female. For you are all one in Christ Jesus.

Galatians 3:28, NLT

But among the Lord's people, women are not independent of men, and men are not independent of women.

1 Corinthians 11:11, NLT

the process of loving my wife in the way she needed to be loved. As a husband and leader of my home, I had to show my wife that I really loved her; I had to make the sacrifice and change my behavior towards her and show it with actions.

I used to get caught up doing things around our home or outside of our home. I hardly ever took out time to spend with her. I believe that I made her feel, at times, that I didn't love her. I knew that I was purposely doing this, and deep down I felt guilty about it. I thought to myself, that if she didn't meet my expectations, I wasn't going to show her any love or affection.

There were many times I felt like giving up on my wife. But, because I knew God, and I loved her, I didn't give up on her. So I had to show her that I loved her with my actions and unconditionally. I had to show her that I loved her no matter what, through the good times and bad times. She shouldn't have to earn my love because we didn't have to earn the love of Christ. He simply loved us.

When you love your wife with sacrificial love, you motivate her to love you the same. We are willing to submit to Christ because of His love and sacrifice, if you want your wife to submit to you, you must love and serve her first.

Christ, being God, came to serve. There's a lesson in that. One of the many things we admire about Christ is His servitude. Imagine the admiration and motivation that our wives would have, if we took on this same attitude. Make sure she knows that you are

Do you inspire your wife? What are ways you could lead your wife inspirationally?

But there is one thing I want you to know: The head of every man is Christ, the head of every woman is man, and the head of Christ is God.

1 Corinthians 11:3, NLT

available to her. That you are willing and able to provide for her in the way she may need. There is nothing wrong with helping her with things that she does on a daily basis. In fact, we read in the Word that Abraham cooked and served, and we see that Esau cooked as well. Men were very involved with the household.

You can also serve your wife with things that can help relax her, and make her feel loved. You shouldn't feel that serving anyone is beneath you. Christ came to serve His most precious creation.

Men, understand that your wife is a gift to you. God said it was not good for man to be alone and He provided you with a very special gift. Not only is your wife a gift for companionship, but she is a suitable helper. Your wife has a title that is worth respect. The Holy Spirit is given the name helper, and as such, you should honor your wife as a suitable helper to you. I definitely cannot do everything that I do without the help of my wife, and for that, I must honor and respect her.

Another way to love like Christ is seeking the best for your wife. Support her in the things that make her happy and bring her joy. She needs just as much fulfillment in other areas of her life just as you do. When you love like Christ loves, oh, how you will see how your wife will love, honor, and respect you. She will happily submit to you because she knows that you are her wise, experienced and discerning protector that she is meant to submit to as her leader.

Do you demonstrate your love? What are ways you show your love to your wife?

_____

_____

_____

_____

_____

_____

_____

_____

_____

_____

_____

_____

_____

Dear children, let's not merely say that we love each other; let us show the truth by our actions.

1 John 3:18, NLT

When you demonstrate trust, she is more than happy to try not to let your trust down. The enemy attacks when one person feels there is a lack of trust. The Word of God in Proverbs 31:10 (page 119) shows us what can be promoted when you instill trust in your wife. Let her know that you trust her, and are happy with her by your side.

Pray for your wife. Encourage her with Biblical truths and daily devotions. When your wife hears you praying for her it will serve as an encouragement to her. She will see that you truly care for her well-being and will learn to trust you more for it.

Help her to feel valued and appreciated. Help her feel how important she is to you, that she is your priority. It is important to vocalize this praise and encouragement. Make sure that you are constantly doing this.

Accept her for all that she is. I know that she may not always do or say the perfect things, but neither will you. Remember that she is probably trying just as hard as you are to make things work out. When you first got together, I am assuming that you did your best to make sure she felt your love and understanding, and it shouldn't be different today.

Let her feel free to come to you in times that she makes mistakes, so that you both can learn to work through them together. Don't continuously point it out, or make her feel guilty. Instead work it out and move forward. Christ doesn't do that with you, so you shouldn't do it with her.

Do you help your wife in areas that may take up lots of her time? What areas can you sacrifice and help to show your affection?

For even the Son of Man came not to be served but to serve others...

Matthew 20:28, NLT

Husband leadership involves more than just giving orders. A husband leader provides spiritual enrichment, encouragement, motivation, selfless service, provision, guidance, and above all, love. God calls us to this, and wants our obedience in this area. Your marriage will get stronger as each day passes if you remember these truths and practice them.

Your marriage will be filled with more love than contempt. There will still be hard times, but with the absolute confirmation of mutual love, you will be able to enjoy a long and happy marriage.

The Third Priority

Although this book is specifically about marriage, children have a place in the discussion of priorities. After God, and then your spouse, the next priority is your children. Parenting is difficult enough by itself. However, you are tasked by God to raise them together, and differences between spouses can make raising children even more difficult.

Parents should work together in the raising of our children. A strong partnership is the best way to demonstrate to your children a united vision where you both share authority together.

Together you should search for the wisdom God provides to instruct and raise your children. You should seek to pray together with your wife, for wisdom for your relationship, for your children,

What are some ways that you can encourage your wife? What are ways you can demonstrate your trust?

Her husband can trust her,
And she will greatly enrich his life.

Proverbs 31:10, NLT

and for everything else that is needed for your home. The stronger your relationship and bond is, the more united you will stand. This bond will serve to build a secure marriage and home life.

When you seek God together, you not only become more united, you will both have the ability to know when each of you is receiving instructions from the Lord. There have been many times my wife and I have been in prayer concerning things with our children, for example. I would be asking the Lord about a concern, and my wife would suddenly answer my prayer with something she felt the Lord was giving her to tell me, and vice versa.

It is valuable for you to seek wisdom through the Word and prayer, but when it concerns your family, time in prayer and Word *together with your wife,* is truly important.

As a husband and a father, it's important that you do your best at not only building your wife up, but also building up your children. You both are their first teachers in every aspect of life. As a father, you can teach them how to love God, how to have relationships, how to communicate, and about kindness, reward, and discipline.

Your devotion to God and to your wife will teach your children immensely. Your devotion to God should also reflect to your wife, your love for her, and your children. It should reflect the type of Christian lifestyle that God calls you to have. If you want for your wife and children to go down the path that God has shown you they should walk, it starts with your devotion to Him. You will be able to give your child the motivation they need, to be who they should be in the Lord, through your personal example. You are their first example.

It isn't enough just to provide for their physical needs. You need to dedicate time to the teaching of your children. You are their first guide in the way they should go with their relationship with the Lord, and guiding their character so that they could be who God intended them to be. Part of this is to love, to teach, and the other is to instill discipline without provoking them.

This will require your actions and your words to align. If you are verbally teaching them to love, then you should be also teaching them to love with your actions. If you are instructing them to read the Word, then it is important that they see you take out time to read the Word. This is important in all areas. If you want your children to learn to rely always on God, then you must demonstrate how you, in your life, rely on the Lord. When you do this, you will not only inspire love and respect from your children, but you will be leading them in the path that they should go.

As men, we are not always very expressive with our love and emotions with our children. When we lack the ability to demonstrate our love, it can be very difficult for a child to accept the things we want to teach them. This includes times of discipline. Discipline is better received when you feel that the person giving it loves and respects you; this is no different for your children.

My children are far from perfect, and there were many things that we learned through trial and error. Looking back on the paths that I chose to take when I allowed God to direct me, helps me to know that I can trust the Word of God. When you see your children applying the things you worked so hard to instill in them, it brings you a sense of peace. It fills your heart with joy, and helps your faith to grow stronger in the Lord.

Your child will learn what is right and wrong from you first. They're not only receiving instruction from you, but they are watching what you do, so you need to do your best at setting an example that they can follow. This is a big responsibility, but God will give you the wisdom and the strength if you ask for it. Above everything that you can teach, is the love that you and only you can provide, and you will forever be blessed.

My father abandoned my mother, and my brother and I, when we were infants. I only have 2 childhood memories of my father and they are not good ones. The things that I was exposed to due to his absence were things that shaped me in ways that were not good for me. It also taught me what *not* to do concerning my wife and children. It wasn't easy being a good father when I didn't have an example of one for many crucial years of my life. So, I was no expert, to say the least. However, I learned to seek after God's wisdom and understanding to be both a better husband and father.

When you lean on God's understanding of how to be a good husband and father, your wife and children will love and respect

What are some ways that you can promote prayer time together with your wife?

_____

_____

_____

_____

_____

_____

_____

_____

_____

_____

_____

My child, listen when your father corrects you.
Don't neglect your mother's instruction.

Proverbs 1:8, NLT

A house is built by wisdom
And becomes strong through good sense.
Through knowledge its rooms are filled
With all sorts of precious riches and valuables.

Proverbs 24:3-4, NLT

Direct your children onto the right path,
And when they are older, they will not leave it.

Proverbs 22:6, NLT

you for all your efforts. I know that some of these things may not be easy to do immediately, and none of us is perfect. In fact, I am still learning each day to be a better husband and father. I can only continuously seek the Lord in prayer and through His Word.

Your priorities are God, wife, and children, but most men value a good friendship. It's good to get support from your Godly friends. This doesn't mean that you have to share anything private or specific, but the Word tells us that a friend is good to help build us up as well. This can be harder for men than it is for women, because men typically don't easily share their struggles and concerns. I struggled with this area, but learned from my wife the importance of building Godly relationships with others.

Choose your friends wisely. God wants you to be able to have friends who will help you in your growth, and who you will help in return. If your friend is counseling anything that is contrary to what God's Word teaches, then he isn't the right counsel. Seek men that are Holy Spirit filled and led. Take time to relax and share with friends; it's good for your own relief and enjoyment.

We need an outlet to be ourselves as men. I often go out to breakfast, or other things that help build good friendships. Find your own forum. Find others in the Kingdom of God that share some of your same interests, and build Godly friendships. This is extremely helpful as an outlet so that you can decompress and be better at home. You can also learn from others and they could learn from you. Remember iron sharpens iron.

What are some ways that you can demonstrate your respect for your wife concerning raising your children together?

_____

_____

_____

_____

_____

_____

_____

_____

Fathers, do not provoke your children to anger by the way you treat them. Rather, bring them up with the discipline and instruction that comes from the Lord.

Ephesians 6:4, NLT

Discipline your son, and he will give you rest;
He will give delight to your heart.

Proverbs 29:17, NLT

The father of the Godly has cause for joy.
What a pleasure to have children who are wise.

Proverbs 23:24, NLT

In Summary

I tell you all of these things because I want you to know that when I speak of these Biblical truths, that I am simply not just stating them. I fully understand the position a man can find himself in, when he is not careful to obey what Christ has to say about how we should live. It can get hard when the enemy tries his best to destroy you and your marriage. However, God has other plans. I was blessed that the Lord opened my eyes to see this.

When you decide to allow God in every area of your life, God will reveal those things that He wants to strip away from you. When this happens, you will find that you will become a better man because God is the one now in charge of your life. It is not easy, nor is it quick, but it is best. God was able to do so many wonderful things in my life personally, when I decided to let go of control, and let Him take control. I was able to see how much God loves me, and what He truly intends for me personally, and for my marriage. With God in the center, you can have the marital relationship that is intended. This is my prayer for you today.

Take some time to list some areas that you would like the Lord to help you be a better husband.

_____

_____

_____

_____

_____

_____

_____

_____

_____

_____

As irons sharpens iron,
so a friend sharpens a friend.

Proverbs 17:17, NLT

Walk with the wise and become wise;
Associate with fools and get in trouble

Proverbs 13:20, NLT

Chapter Three - Discussion Questions

Are there any areas in your life where you may not be fulfilling your role as a husband? What will you do to improve in these areas? How can your wife help you to improve?

_____

_____

_____

_____

_____

_____

_____

_____

_____

_____

_____

_____

_____

_____

Chapter Three – Take Action!

Compare your answer to the question on page 115, with that of your wife's answer on women's page 101. Decide together which are the most important ways that you each will show your love and respect for the other, and commit to showing your appreciation in these ways.

_____

_____

_____

_____

_____

_____

_____

_____

_____

_____

_____

Chapter 4

TEAMWORK

I appeal to you…
that you be united in the same mind and the same judgment.
1 Corinthians 1:10, ESV

So far we've done some hard work, and you're halfway there. This construction project is working out fine. To recap, the blueprints have been designed, the foundation has been laid, and everyone is operating in their perspective function.

However, a construction job also requires some team effort. There are roles and work that has to be properly executed by each person individually, but there are other things that take more than one person to be able to accomplish. Things that can only be done with teamwork.

In case you haven't realized it yet, you and your spouse are both a team, and must function as one unit. You each have your individual role or function, but teamwork is what's going to make this construction project be successful. It's only through harmonious teamwork that a project is completed.

Teams don't always work in harmony. Troubles come and cause contention between the team. The team must find ways to see past their differences and continue forward with the project. At other times, troubles or obstacles come against the project altogether and the team must make every effort to do their part to save the project and the team members themselves.

Well, this is exactly what happens in your marriage. You get into disagreements, or face issues or problems that cause arguments and strife in your marriage. Or the enemy comes up against your marriage in order to destroy it. The enemy tries his best to ruin your marriage. He hates what your marriage stands for and wants nothing more than to destroy it. He is against your union, and against the harmony and stability of your children and your home.

Conflict Happens

First, you must know that conflict in marriage is absolutely normal. Conflict will always exist because we are all different human beings, with different thoughts, ideas, and opinions. It's not the conflict that defines you. It's how you resolve the conflict that will ultimately speak about who you are in Christ. Sometimes conflict is fairly easy to resolve. At other times, conflict seems like it's impossible to move past. Be encouraged and know that you can do all things through Christ who strengthens you, and this includes resolving conflict.

There are many types of challenges that cause the conflict that most couples face. Challenges with finances, challenges with raising children, challenges with in-laws, challenges with friends, work, school, etc. Challenges when you disagree on where to go, or what to do. Depending on how strongly you feel about a certain thing, this can raise conflict. Other reasons that conflict can start are that your expectations are not met, when you feel unappreciated, or undervalued. When you feel that your rights, or what you believe that you deserve, have been violated. It is hard to move past these types of disagreements and disappointments.

Conflict can be difficult and straining, but conflict resolution can cause the conflict to be a blessing in disguise. It can help you to understand each other better and gives you an opportunity to grow. The Word of God speaks to you about how conflict helps increase your faith, but it also helps to mature you. When conflict strikes, try to learn from the experience.

I know that trying to learn from a disagreement is easier said than done, but it is possible to take from your disagreements things that can be positive for your relationship. As you grow together through each conflict, you will learn more about each other. You'll also learn to be a bit more patient each time. Each time a bit more understanding.

What are the areas of your marriage you feel you struggle with the most? What are some ways that you can make improvements?

_____

_____

_____

_____

_____

_____

_____

_____

_____

_____

_____

_____

Consider it pure joy, my brothers and sisters, whenever you face trials of many kinds, because you know that the testing of your faith produces perseverance. Let perseverance finish its work so that you may be mature and complete, not lacking anything.

James 1:2-4 NIV

Who's Your Enemy?

Another important thing that you must know is that your spouse is not your enemy. Your one and only enemy is Satan. You have to make sure that you know and remember this fact when you are in the middle of a conflict. Don't treat your spouse as your enemy; your spouse is certainly not your enemy. It can feel as though as you are sleeping with the enemy at times, but you must know that it's not so. Your true enemy is the Devil, and he will try to bring everything he can to come against you and your spouse.

Sometimes you can get so angry and treat your spouse as though they are your enemy, when in fact, you are told to love your spouse. For men, this love is an unconditional and sacrificial love that is compared to how Christ loves the church, and for women, a love that is compared to how the church loves Christ.

This is a tall order, but it is possible if you keep Christ in the center of your marriage. You must take the steps and actions necessary to love your spouse in the way that God wants us to love. Your marriage is a reflection of the relationship between Christ and the church.

Think about the ways you may have treated your spouse and ask yourself if these are ways that Christ would treat the church, or if these are ways that the church would treat Christ.

Have you ever treated your spouse like your enemy? What are some ways you can avoid this in the future?

_____

_____

_____

_____

_____

_____

_____

_____

_____

_____

_____

For we are not fighting against flesh-and-blood enemies, but against evil rulers and authorities of the unseen world, against mighty powers in this dark world, and against evil spirits in the heavenly places.

Ephesians 6:12 NLT

No one is perfect, but you must strive to live Christ-like. The first person after God that you should be striving to love unconditionally is your spouse.

Why Conflict?

Conflict occurs because people all have different thoughts and ideas. Conflict also occurs because of your desires. The first conflict occurred in the Garden of Eden. The serpent tempted Eve, and the fruit became desirable to her. Through that desire, she reached out and ate it. When Adam also ate the fruit, they came to understand about good and evil, and they were no longer living in innocence. Sin entered the world. Sin causes the communication lines to be broken between man and woman, and between all of us and God.

There were consequences because of the sin that was committed in the Garden of Eden, and these consequences cause conflict. There is conflict between Satan and man. God, at that moment, did provide a solution with the promise of Christ when He said that the seed of the woman would crush Satan's head. Nonetheless, there is conflict.

Sin is the root cause to all conflict. Some may say desire, but Eve's desire is not what caused their eyes to be opened. Their eyes were opened only after they ate, not after they desired. The desire or temptation will come, but it is what you do when it does come

Think back to your first conflict together. Do you feel you have grown since then? How?

_____

_____

_____

_____

_____

_____

_____

The woman was convinced. She saw that the tree was beautiful and its fruit looked delicious, and she wanted the wisdom it would give her. So she took some of the fruit and ate it. Then she gave some to her husband, who was with her, and he ate it, too. At that moment their eyes were opened, and they suddenly felt shame at their nakedness. So they sewed fig leaves together to cover themselves.

Genesis 3:6-7, NLT

I will put enmity between you and the woman, and between your offspring and her offspring; he shall bruise your head, and you shall bruise his heel.

Genesis 3:15, ESV

that matters. When you desire something specific and it is not provided, this can cause emotions to rise. It can cause anger, disappointment, or hurt.

There is nothing wrong with emotion, but sometimes the actions you take because of an emotional feeling can be wrong. Anger is a normal feeling. You get angry when you feel that your spouse has violated your rights, your needs, and your self-worth. It is not wrong to get angry, but you must be careful of your actions when you do get angry. You can't allow yourself to be ruled by your anger, because this can lead to sin.

Anger is a very strong emotion. It can serve in positive ways. You can use anger as a motivation to get things resolved or do things better. For example, you can be angry that something was not completed, and then you decide to complete it.

Anger can also lead to things that can harm you or your relationship. Out of anger, you can do or say harmful things to your spouse. Anger can be cause for you to house bitterness in your heart, or in the heart of your spouse. Anger can lead to depression, resentfulness, isolation, and other things that can cause not only conflict in your marriage, but also put a strain on your communication and relationship with each other, and more importantly, your communication and relationship with God.

Let's look at the definition of conflict. Conflict is a serious disagreement or argument. It doesn't always *start* with something serious. Sometimes conflict starts out with the silliest or the most

Do you let your anger get the best of you? What are some things you need to change to avoid this anger?

_____

_____

_____

_____

_____

_____

_____

_____

_____

What causes quarrels and what causes fights among you? Is it not this, that your passions are at war within you? You desire and do not have, so you murder. You covet and cannot obtain, so you fight and quarrel. You do not have, because you do not ask.
James 4:1-2, ESV

And "don't sin by letting anger control you...
Ephesians 4:26, NLT

insignificant things, and then escalates to something bigger, and before you know it, is has blown out of proportion. This can occur when there is stress from other issues, or when you keep things inside and don't communicate them. Then when something comes up that is small, it escalates into something else.

In a previous chapter, I have shared with you some of my thoughts on what it takes to develop your relationship and communication with God, and then each other. You can use some of these thoughts to be better at resolving conflict.

Your relationship and communication with God will help you to be wiser about the things you need to resolve with each other. Better communication and relationship with each other will also help for a much smoother resolution process when conflict occurs. There are other things that you must be ready to do, and ready to accomplish in your relationship if you want to bring conflict resolution into your marriage in a better way.

Confronting

So far, communication has been a key topic throughout these sessions, and it is no different here. Communication is the foundation. I shared with you about how each of us has a different communication style. Sometimes, because of the different styles, and the lack of the understanding of these different styles, your spouse may be offended, which can cause hurt, pain or anger. Even if you know the communication style of your spouse, sometimes they can still end up offended. Angela and I have suffered many times in our own marriage because of this very thing.

I know what he means, but I still can't help feeling hurt or angry when he expresses himself in a certain way, and vice-versa. This is mainly because we're emotional beings.

Some people are more emotional than others are, but none of us are robots, and we don't analytically compute every detail. Some days you can shrug it off and keep moving, and some days you just feel like you can't deal with it. This is absolutely normal, because human beings are imperfect. You must choose to make the appropriate responses to your spouse in order to avoid this as much as possible. Try your best to be understanding and patient.

But sometimes this is just not enough. Sometimes you have to communicate your feelings and what he or she is doing that is causing you pain, hurt, or anger.

You have to confront your spouse with what you believe they have done against you. The Lord knew that there would be difficulty, and He provides the solution.

Matthew 18:15 (page 143) says to confront the other person, but then it also adds, "If the person listens and confesses it, you have won that person back". This is important because this shows that there is a dynamic to this. If you are the confronter, you must be open and honest, but if you are the offender, you must be willing to listen, and confess. In other words, accept or take responsibility for what you have said or done that has caused the offense.

This could be difficult because you may feel that you're not guilty of what you are being confronted with. However, perception is key. Remember that people have different communication styles, and at times, certain communication styles can be misunderstood. Therefore, it's important to listen to how the other person feels, and accept that you may have provoked that feeling. Even if it was unintentional, you should accept and apologize for it.

Confronting should be done in love. You should speak truthfully and honestly, but choose your words carefully. You should not look to accuse your spouse. Remember that perception can be at play. You might assume that your spouse meant to offend or harm you; however, it may not be so. You will need to ensure that you do your best at not offending your spouse when you choose to confront them.

When you confront your spouse, not only do you have to do it in love, but also you have to do it respectfully. Your goal should not be to let them know how bad they did, but to help them to be better. To edify, encourage, and help them.

You may be confronting them because they've hurt you, but your goal should not be to hurt them back. You need to make sure that you're not doing this with an underlying motive. Be sure that you are solely doing it to resolve the conflict and to help build up your spouse.

If you have ever confronted your spouse, was it always in love? List anything you may change in how you do this in the future.

_____

_____

_____

_____

_____

_____

_____

_____

_____

_____

If another believer sins against you, go privately and point out the offense. If the other person listens and confesses it, you have won that person back.

Matthew 18:15 NLT

There may be times that your spouse may have actually meant to hurt or offend you. Consider why this is the case. Usually when a person chooses to do this, it's because they have been hurt or offended. Even if they are purposely doing this, when you confront your spouse, remain calm and express yourself respectfully and in love. One thing I learned from my aunt and now always say is, "when there is a fire, water can put it out." You both can't be fire, when one is fire, then the one should take the role of water.

There are those who don't like to confront their spouse. They keep things that bother them to themselves. This is not good at all. You may think that you are helping the situation because you don't want to cause an argument, or offend your spouse. In fact, you are not only doing harm to yourself; you are also doing an injustice to your spouse. Keeping things bottled up can cause emotional and physical harm to yourself.

When you don't resolve the problem, you don't move beyond it. This can lead to you exploding with anger when your bottle is full to the brim. It can lead to isolation, which interferes with your communication and relationship.

The injustice to your spouse is that you could be holding this offense against them, and without giving them an opportunity to know what they are doing, or even make it right so that they do not continue to do it. When they are unaware that something they are doing is bothering you, you cannot hold them solely responsible for every time they do it again.

Do you take correction well? Are you open to your spouse pointing out ways to improve? How can you be more receiving and understanding?

_____

_____

_____

_____

_____

_____

_____

_____

_____

_____

Instead, we will speak the truth in love, growing in every way more and more like Christ, who is the head of his body, the church.

Ephesians 4:15, NLT

Don't use foul or abusive language. Let everything you say be good and helpful, so that your words will be an encouragement to those who hear them.

Ephesians 4:29, NLT

There are times that you feel that you shouldn't have to confront your spouse because they should know already. Or because it is not your responsibility to point out their flaws. Or they don't deserve for you to make peace with them. You feel that they are the ones at fault, and so you deserve for them to come to you and apologize. I understand this feeling all too well. In fact, there were times when I would sit and argue with God about how I hated to have to be the one making peace, and how it wasn't fair, and that Luis should be the one to come to me.

There were two things I had to learn from these feelings. First, Jesus made himself clear when he said that if you are offended you should go to your brother and point out his fault. He didn't say to wait on the other person to come and make it right with you. Know that confronting your spouse is an act of obedience.

The second thing I had to learn was that my complaining to God about how Luis should be the one coming to me was prideful. Pride is such an ugly thing. Although I would eventually be the one to make peace, deep down inside I felt that it should have been him. I had to put those feelings to the side, and I had to swallow my pride.

God does not want pride within us. When Christ tells us to confront our offender and point out their flaws, not only is He telling us to do this so that we would have peace, but He is telling us to do this so that we can avoid being prideful, or to hold bitterness, anger and other feelings in our hearts.

Do you effectively communicate how you feel? List ways you can improve your communication with your spouse.

_____

_____

_____

_____

_____

_____

_____

_____

_____

_____

Get rid of all bitterness, rage, anger, harsh words, and slander, as well as all types of evil behavior. Instead, be kind to each other, tenderhearted, forgiving one another, just as God through Christ has forgiven you.

Ephesians 4:31-32, NLT

Sometimes pride may lead you to blame your spouse, while at the same time rationalizing away your own flaws and justifying your actions based on their actions. This is the same blame game that Adam and Eve did when they first committed sin, and mankind has been doing it ever since. It is a defense mechanism. But in order for you to work through conflict and be forgiving toward your spouse, you need to do less of pointing fingers and expecting them to change. Instead, do more self-reflection, and start by changing yourself.

One of the ways a marriage is going to be able to be strengthened through conflict, is if each individual takes responsibility to make needed improvements in themselves. You shouldn't try to change your spouse; you should only try to change yourself. Work on yourself, your own flaws, your own attitudes, your own weaknesses, not your spouse's. Your focus needs to be on all the wonderful, positive, and great things about your spouse. It might help to go back to the moment you first fell in love. It's up to you to forgive, and bring peace to your marriage.

Forgiveness

God wants to get rid of all bitterness, rage, and anger because it is not good for you. These feelings, although not sinful, can lead you to doing sinful things. It can lead you to house these feelings in your heart. You cannot operate properly with these feelings held

Do you act out of anger or pride? What are ways you can improve in this area?

_____

_____

_____

_____

_____

_____

_____

_____

_____

_____

_____

_____

Then Peter came to him and asked, "Lord, how often should I forgive someone who sins against me? Seven times?" "No, not seven times," Jesus replied, "but seventy times seven!"

Matthew 18:21-22, NLT

inside. When Christ tells you to settle these faults with your spouse, He is doing it for your own good.

Instead, God wants you to be kind, tenderhearted and forgiving to one another, just as He forgave you. You didn't deserve forgiveness and yet Christ forgives you for your sins. If you receive forgiveness from the Lord, you should forgive your spouse. It can feel quite tiresome at times when you continuously have to forgive them for the same thing. Maybe it's an area they struggle with like a bad habit, or something that was taught to them growing up. Patience is needed, and forgiveness is a blessing for you both. God forgives you and continues forgiving you daily.

Your forgiveness toward each other should not be conditional. It's not easy, and in fact, it can be very difficult at times, depending on the offense. You must seek the Lord and His guidance when you are having difficulty forgiving your spouse's offense. This does not give your spouse permission to offend you repeatedly. Each of you must strive to be better and not commit the offense again, especially after you have been advised of how the offense is harmful. However, when we forgive, we are demonstrating love.

Sometimes we may feel that forgiving a certain offense is impossible. However, this is not true. Love covers many things. Again, this doesn't mean that it's easy, but it also doesn't mean that it's impossible. You have to seek the Lord and He will help you to forgive.

Choose to forgive. Once you choose to obey the Lord by forgiving, ask Him to help you forgive. Forgiveness is not an instant cure for the hurt, but it is the first step in that direction. God wants us to be free of all the hurt, and He offers forgiveness as a path to that freedom. The path to healing starts with forgiveness. You have to choose and take the right steps and actions to demonstrate that you truly have forgiven. It is not simply by words, but by your actions that you are going to show your forgiveness toward your spouse.

When granting forgiveness, make sure that you specifically state why you are forgiving them. Don't speak in generalities, which can cause your spouse to feel as though you have not truly forgiven them. If you're unclear, they may assume that you have only forgiven him or her for some of the things and not all.

When forgiving your spouse you should also accept any fault of your own in the situation. While they may have been the aggressor, you may have had a hand in provoking that aggression, whether you meant to or not. Being transparent and owning up to your own flaws can help your spouse not only to accept what you are saying, but also be thankful that you pointed out the flaw.

Lastly, when granting forgiveness make sure that you don't hold on to the offense. The idea is to forgive and move on. You may not be able to forget immediately, but that should be between you and God. Don't constantly bring up an offense that you have already forgiven. This can be harmful and strain your relationship.

When you commit to always forgiving each other, it becomes easier to ask forgiveness before it gets to the point of discussion. Try not to wait for your spouse to come to you with their hurt. If you know that you acted or spoke to them in harmful ways, then own up to what you have done, and ask for forgiveness.

This is so important to God, that He would rather you not go to Him in worship until you have reconciled with your spouse. This also shows your spouse how much you love them, and how much you are truly sorry.

Don't hold back from asking for forgiveness when you need to. The enemy can cause guilt to bring shame and condemnation to yourself due to a way you have acted or things you may have said to your spouse. Don't let the enemy take hold of situations that can be settled with simple communication. Guilt can lead to bitterness and resentment.

Asking for forgiveness can be helpful for you and definitely for your spouse. It can provoke in your spouse the thought of your consideration, responsibility, and commitment to the relationship. Not that it would guarantee that the forgiveness would be immediate, but if you take the first step, it can help in a big way for the healing process.

When you ask for forgiveness make sure you specifically state why you need to be forgiven. A transparent confession is always best. Admitting to what you have said or done is important for the

Are you holding things against your spouse? What are some things you can offer your spouse forgiveness for?

_____

_____

_____

_____

_____

_____

_____

_____

_____

_____

Most important of all, continue to show deep love for each other, for love covers a multitude of sins.

1 Peter 4:8, NLT

bearing with one another and, if one has a complaint against another, forgiving each other; as the Lord has forgiven you, so you also must forgive.

Colossians 3:13, ESV

healing to begin. When you ask for forgiveness in general, you may not be actually receiving forgiveness for something specifically and that offense can still linger.

Make sure that you are sincere with your apology. Be sincerely remorseful for what you have said or done. More hurt can be caused if your spouse feels that you are not sincere. Also, saying the actual words, "Would you forgive me?" is very powerful. This can open the doors to healing as well.

Remember to forgive yourself. If you have done all you can to ask for forgiveness, make sure that you forgive yourself. The enemy wants to hold you down with feelings of regret and condemnation. God forgave you, your spouse forgave you, and then it's time for *you* to forgive you.

Finally, know when to choose your battles. Be careful not to correct your spouse for every assumed offense. Pause before you react too quickly, to ensure that you fully understand the situation. We need to make sure that we are seeking the Lord's direction in these things before reacting.

There is wisdom in refraining from speaking sometimes. Remember that you and your spouse are a team, and sometimes it is fitting to take one for the team. If you know that what was done to you is not always done and you are sure that it was only because of stress or the circumstance, then keep it. Take one for the team.

Are you aware of ways that you may have offended your spouse? What are some things you feel you may need forgiveness for?

_____

_____

_____

_____

_____

_____

_____

_____

_____

_____

_____

So if you are offering your gift at the altar and there remember that your brother has something against you, leave your gift there before the altar and go. First be reconciled to your brother, and then come and offer your gift.

Matthew 5:23-24, ESV

Pointing out someone's flaws all the time can be harmful. Women are stereotypically considered to be nagging, but husbands can also be quarrelsome. Make sure that you are not pointing out someone's flaws just because you can. Seek the Lord before you do. To confront or not to confront, that is the question. Well, the answer is, ask the Lord. Always seek the Lord before you confront.

In Summary

Conflict is a difficult area and there isn't a way to avoid it. However, through conflict and its resolution, we can become closer in our relationship if we choose to learn from what we have experienced. Out of love for your spouse, make sure that you keep the lines of communication open so that conflict resolution can occur. Make sure that you both are communicating your hurts, and your apologies to each other. Pray for one another, love and respect one another, and through it all, always seek the Lord's guidance.

Have you given your spouse a hard time with something in particular? Is there an area your spouse struggles with that you can offer more kindness instead of pointing out his or her flaws constantly?

_____

_____

_____

_____

_____

_____

_____

_____

_____

_____

When words are many, transgression is not lacking, but whoever restrains his lips is prudent.

Proverbs 10:19, ESV

Better to live in a desert than with a quarrelsome and nagging wife.

Proverbs 21:19, NIV

Chapter Four - Discussion Questions

How do you communicate to your wife that she has hurt you? Are there ways that you can respond more positively?

_____

_____

_____

_____

_____

_____

_____

_____

_____

_____

_____

_____

_____

Chapter Four – Take Action!

Talk to your wife about something that has been troubling you. Listen as your wife tells you about something that is troubling her. Don't be defensive or unwilling to listen. Ask for or grant forgiveness, if needed. Determine together how you both can improve in these areas.

_____

_____

_____

_____

_____

_____

_____

_____

_____

_____

_____

_____

Chapter 5

DÉCOR

...love the Lord your God with all your heart...
...Love your neighbor as yourself...
Mark 12:30-32, NLT

You're getting closer to finishing the construction project. Right about now, the project is looking good, but there is still some work to do. All the actual building is complete, and it is time for some final additions. Once the structure of a new building is up the fun part begins. You are working as a team to get to some of the fine details. It's time to decorate the interior. This is the moment to take some thought and time to make everything look and feel just right. Choose all the details that will go into every room, and make sure that it looks phenomenal.

In our intimate relationships, it should be the same way, and in this building project, you have two main focus points to decorate. Every chapter of this book so far, has stressed the importance of your relationship with God. Always put God first, and when you do, everything else will be successful. Christ should be in the center of your marriage, and in the topic of intimacy, it is the same.

Once again, I will be talking to you man to man, and my wife will be talking to your wife. Because this topic covers sex, it can be a bit controversial. Some may not be comfortable talking about sexual intimacy, but nonetheless it is an important part of your marriage so to leave it out would be a big mistake.

Intimacy with God

There are different sides of intimacy. There is spiritual intimacy, and physical intimacy. With God, we have spiritual intimacy. Previous chapters discussed prayer, seeking God through His Word, seeking His direction for your marriage, and understanding His plan and purpose for you in your marriage.

God loves you more than you can comprehend. God loves you with a deep love and He makes sure that you know that throughout His Word. The problem is that sometimes as men, we have trouble expressing our love to others. This includes our love of God. You have to start an intimate relationship with God and express all the things you have within you. You might not be as emotional as your wife is, and so sometimes, this can be difficult. There are so many things that you live through as a man, and so many things that society tells you about what a "real" man does and does not do, that you may not even realize how it affects you.

What happens is that when you continue to act in a non-emotional way, you actually hold in things that you need to let go. I grew up seeing many things that sometimes I wish I could un-see. Those things caused me to build walls around my heart. Women, not all, but most women tend to release many emotions to help them cope. But men tend to keep things bottled up, and it makes for a tough exterior, and then this becomes a barrier to their heart.

You must release yourself to the Lord so that you can have the intimate relationship you were meant to have with both the Lord and your wife. You must allow those walls to come down. The people of Jericho had strong walls, and kept their gates tightly shut because they were afraid of the Israelites. They were correct to be afraid because the Lord was on the opposite side.

For you this is not the case, the Lord is not on the opposing side, and there is no need to keep your gates shut and the walls up. On the contrary, there is a flood of blessing that awaits when you decide to open the gates and tear down the walls.

This is exactly what I had to do. I had to release everything I had to the Lord. This allowed me to have a better relationship with Him. I was able to learn to love myself, which allowed me to love others better, especially my wife. I can't love my wife with that sacrificial love like Christ, if I have my walls up. I was able to release everything by putting my trust and my life in Him.

I had to seek the Lord intimately. I had to search for Him privately alone, and just pour my heart out to Him. I learned that

Do you have issues expressing yourself emotionally? Think about what reasons may be holding you back.

He was waiting for me to do that my whole life. I felt God's love, and He proved to be my friend.

Jesus shared everything with the disciples, and through His Word, He shares everything with us. This is how you become a friend; you become a friend when you are able to share, and Jesus wants to be your friend. He wants you to confide in Him. All those things that you have wrapped up inside, that you learned men were not supposed to share, you must share them with the Lord.

When you're able to be open with the Lord, you'll be able to be open with your wife. When you engage in sexual relations with your wife, you're revealing your most private side. You're showing your wife a side of you that no one else sees. Your sexual relationship with your wife can be better if you're able to also share other sides of you. This is possible if you first start with God.

The reason why I say to first start with God is because no one can do what God can do. All those things that you have bottled up can be released to God, and not only will God listen, but God can heal and restore wherever it is needed. God can help you to move past the things that you need to move past. This healing and restoration sets you free to be more intimate with your wife.

Intimacy with your Wife

The reason that healing and restoration helps with sexual intimacy is that in order for the sexual intimacy part to be great, the

God is your friend. List any unresolved issues distracting you from attaining a deeper spiritual intimacy with the Lord?

_____

_____

_____

_____

_____

_____

_____

_____

_____

_____

I no longer call you slaves, because a master doesn't confide in his slaves. Now you are my friends, since I have told you everything the Father told me.

John 15:15, NLT

emotional intimacy must be even greater. When there is a lacking in your sexual intimacy, it is usually a sign that there is another underlying problem. Something else is wrong and it is spilling into this area. This is because women are different from men. Women are emotional beings and must feel emotionally attached to you in order to engage in sex properly. I say properly because sometimes they can do the act just to fulfill their duty, but not really be "there" with you.

Women can bring their entire day into the bedroom. Because women are relational and inclusive, everything that is affecting them emotionally and physically can affect them when they are intimate with you. They can be easily distracted and it can affect your intimate time together. Your wife needs to feel loved, appreciated, and secure by you. Men are more easily stimulated, while loving words and a loving attitude stimulate women.

It is important that you build emotional intimacy with your wife first. Building emotional intimacy will bring you closer to your wife, and will enhance your sexual intimacy with her. According to an article describing the development and validation of the Emotional Intimacy Scale, the authors state that "emotional intimacy involves a perception of closeness to another that allows sharing of personal feelings, accompanied by expectations of understanding, affirmation, and demonstrations of caring."[3]

---

[3] Sinclair, V., & Dowdy, S. (2005, Winter). Development and Validation of the Emotional Intimacy Scale. *Journal of Nursing Measurement*, pp. 193-206.

If you want to have a successful marriage, you must be mindful of your wife's emotional and physical needs. Your wife expects and desires that you fulfill those needs. Sometimes, because of lack of communication, busyness, tiredness, and disagreements, you might tend to disregard her needs. You must make it a priority to build emotional intimacy with your wife.

If you don't build emotional intimacy with your wife, it can lead to dissention. It's going to take communication, encouragement, devotion, and praying together to build emotional intimacy. You have to build a personal and deep connection with your wife. You do this through different ways but they are all needed in order for the connection to be strong.

First, there is communication. Communication with each other and with the Lord. You should make every effort to spend time in the Word, and in prayer with your wife. You will strengthen your marriage through the help of the Holy Spirit. Make sure that you are taking the necessary time to be in the Lord's presence. Intimate time in the Lord, together, as a couple, will help make your bond stronger.

Your wife's physical needs include sexual intimacy, but that isn't all there is to her physical needs. They also include her wellbeing and taking care of her person. It also means being considerate of her physical rest. Sometimes you can forget that your wife can become physically exhausted. Do your best to help in every way you can to ensure that she does not overexert herself.

Keeping a home, working, and raising a family can sometimes be overwhelming, and as a leader, you need to be understanding and know when it's time to intervene for her wellbeing.

There is no shame in helping in the home. In fact, the responsibility of the home is for you both. Society has placed the burden of the home on the woman. It made sense when most of the women were homemakers and the husbands were the only ones working. However, today women share the load of helping to bring financial means to the household. Shouldn't this mean that men should now share with the load of the household since the women are sharing the load through having secular jobs?

Helping in the home and with children cannot only be a blessing for your wife; it can also bless your children. Helping your wife with some of the domestic responsibilities is a way to demonstrate your love for her. It gives her the message that you are both working together. If she sees how much you care about the things that need to be done in the household, you can motivate her in other ways to demonstrate her love back to you.

For every area of your marriage function properly, you must invite God into the middle of your marriage. Through spiritual intimacy, you'll adopt the fruit of the Spirit, which will help you be better individuals to each other. Choose to invite God in the center of your marriage, and you'll see Him work in all areas.

What areas can you be helpful to give your wife some added rest?

We went over communication in chapter 2, concerning the building of your relationship and companionship, but communication is also important for emotional and sexual intimacy with your wife. If your wife doesn't feel emotionally connected with you through communication, she will not be able to connect with you physically.

In the verse on page 171, the woman is describing her desire for the young man, who is both her lover and her friend. If you want your wife to desire you physically, you must be attractive to her emotionally. A friend is someone who she can share with, someone who will listen to her, and be there in her time of personal need.

You need to build a friendship with your wife. When you first got together, you made your best effort to court her and made sure that you listened to her speak and spent time with her.

After marriage, it should be no different, with the exception that now you are a couple. There's a larger reason to care for her even more than before. If you want to continue being her friend, you need to communicate your feelings and make sure that you are listening to hers.

Be and encouragement to your wife. To encourage means to give someone support or confidence. To build and lift her up. When you do, you are not only helping her, but you are helping yourself, because she is your teammate. She is your partner.

Are you still a friend with your wife? Do you interact with her other than sexually? What are ways that you can build companionship?

His mouth is sweetness itself; he is desirable in every way.
Such, O women of Jerusalem, is my lover, my friend.
Song of Solomon 5:16, NLT

As partners, you are able to help each other succeed, and are able to grow closer. And with the Lord being in the center, your marriage cord will not be easily broken. The Word says that two people lying close together can keep each other warm. The bond that is built by you and your wife through communication and encouragement will warm up your marriage in every area, including the bedroom.

Emotional intimacy also involves you demonstrating and vocalizing your love for her. You have to show her with your actions that you care for her, that she is the most important part of your life. Eye contact, physical touch, and attention can help demonstrate your love to her. Small thoughtful acts, such as surprises, gifts, and other considerations can help to make her feel special to you. I would cook dinner, iron her clothes, or simply tell her to relax when she got home. I sometimes would buy or make her favorite dessert. There are many actions you can take to demonstrate your love for her. Find out what your wife likes, and then make it a point to do it for her.

Demonstrating your love, means that you're proving your love by showing how you feel, or by example. Give your wife examples of your love for her. This is done by doing things for her that you know will make her happy. Bring home a favorite thing from time to time, do something for her that you know she'll like, or simply relieve her of some of her daily duties when you can.

Sexual intimacy for your wife can be wrapped up in how encouraged she feels by you. Your support and confidence in her can promote trust and comfort. Name some things you can do to promote this in your wife.

Two people are better off than one, for they can help each other succeed. If one person falls, the other can reach out and help. But someone who falls alone is in real trouble. Likewise, two people lying close together can keep each other warm. But how can one be warm alone? A person standing alone can be attacked and defeated, but two can stand back-to-back and conquer. Three are even better, for a triple-braided cord is not easily broken.

Ecclesiastes 4:9-12, NLT

Fifty years ago, it was the norm for the husband to work outside the home, and perhaps work in the yard or his workshop on the weekends. It was the wife's job to take care of all domestic tasks, fully responsible for all homemaking and all of the care of any children. Even after women began working outside the home, they were often still the primary homemaker and caregiver.

You need to understand that when you do chores at home, you are not "helping her" with the housework. Actually, you're sharing in the work that both of you are equally responsible for. Whether both of you work outside the home, or one of you is the homemaker, remember that being a homemaker has no breaks, and can be mentally and physically exhausting, just like employment can be. Since for women sex is mostly mental, if she is exhausted because you're not participating in taking care of your home, it will be hard for her to have the desire to be intimate with you.

Demonstrate genuine affection. Make sure she feels loved and desired. Your wife needs to know that she is desired by you. She should both feel and hear from you regularly how beautiful and attractive she is.

After the years have set in, it's easy to take for granted what you have. The years can cause you to become stagnant in your affection towards your wife. You might fail to show interest in her. You should make a point to show affection towards her, not only in the bedroom, but also in other ways. Thoughtful, flirtatious acts, and affectionate physical touches demonstrate your love

List some small details that you can do to demonstrate your love to your wife.

_____

_____

_____

_____

_____

_____

_____

_____

_____

_____

_____

Dear children, let's not merely say that we love each other; let us show the truth by our actions.

1 John 3:18, NLT

Your wife needs your physical touch. Hugging, cuddling, and holding are demonstrations of intimacy for your wife. For example, sitting on the couch as you watch a movie, holding her close can help to make her feel wanted and attractive. Using affectionate words, and telling her how much you love her and how beautiful she is, can help to connect with her emotionally and sexually.

Don't stop dating your wife. Don't stop romancing your wife. Remember what you did to win her love and affection in the first place. Those acts should not cease. Just because you have her as your wife, doesn't mean that you stop trying to win her love daily. This doesn't mean that you have to do anything extravagant. While extravagant is good, simple daily signs of affection and love are what will keep her love for you strong.

I made that mistake and it put a strain on my marriage. At one point, I failed at making sure my wife knew how much I appreciated and loved her. Then I failed at making sure she knew how beautiful she still was to me. I failed to show her compassion, consideration, and understanding. Moreover, when you do this, you are not honoring your wife, and when you do not honor your wife, your prayers can be hindered.

Sometimes when you've had a long day, your wife can be an easy target. But, you must not forget that although she may be weaker than you are physically, she is your equal. She is the one God gave you as not only a helper, but a strong and capable helper.

Physical touch, beautiful words are helpful to increase your wife's interest in sexual intimacy. What are some things you know your wife would like you to show or do?

_____

_____

_____

_____

_____

_____

_____

_____

_____

_____

_____

_____

Love each other with genuine affection, and take delight in honoring each other.

Romans 12:10, NLT

You must value her and let her know you value her. Treat her properly and not harshly. Make sure to always to speak to her in loving ways, with understanding.

Sometimes words can cause the most hurt. Try to be mindful of how you speak to her. The enemy is in the business of using words to cause confusion and contention. It was with his words that he fooled and convinced Eve in the garden. It is all that much easier for the enemy to use harsh words to cause contention and strife in your marital relationship. Harsh actions are even worse. This is something as a man of God that is truly not acceptable, and should be something that you work on intently if it is an area of weakness.

The Bible actually states "never" to treat your wife harshly. Remember that you are to love her as Christ loved the church, and Christ is never harsh with you. On the contrary, Christ loves you unconditionally, is kind, and considerate with you. You should be the same way with your wife.

One way that men can be harsh with words is to say things that go against her person. You have to be careful not to offend your wife when it concerns her physical body. She may go through some bodily changes after having children, or with age and you should consider her just as beautiful as the first time you saw her.

Although her physical appearance may be different, her beauty is now much deeper than just her physical looks. This is why your

Have you been guilty of harsh treatment? List ways that you can be better in your treatment toward your wife.

_____

_____

_____

_____

_____

_____

_____

_____

In the same way, you husbands must give honor to your wives. Treat your wife with understanding as you live together. She may be weaker than you are, but she is your equal partner in God's gift of new life. Treat her as you should so your prayers will not be hindered.

1 Peter 3:7, NLT

Husbands, love your wives and never treat them harshly.

Colossians 3:19, NLT

love should run much deeper than that. It is now on a more spiritual intimate level. You connect with her in a deeper way than just your physical bodies. You both have endured through years of changes, but have also grown knowing each other more.

When you make your wife feel as though you don't find her physically attractive, it can cause emotional strain and insecurities. This can affect your sexual intimacy with her. In order for your wife to enjoy her time with you sexually, you need to make sure that she is emotionally connected to you. This connection can be broken through this type of offense.

The Word of God gives you a blessing that you might always be captivated by her love. Captivated means to attract and hold interest and attention. You're to hold interest in your wife. Make sure that she knows just how beautiful she continues to be. Never criticize any part of her body. You don't want to be the cause of insecurity in your wife. This can lead to her shutting herself in, and could damage both emotional and physical intimacy.

Instead, be kind, and make sure to compliment her often. If she is having issues with weight or other things that are unhealthy for her, it is not motivation to tell her in harsh ways. Instead, tell her that you want both of you to be healthier so that you both can have a longer, healthy marriage. That you want to make sure that you are both taking care of yourselves, and that it would be an encouragement to you if she would join you for support. Do these things without hurting her. The result will be best for you both.

Kind words, and words of affirmation of her beauty are also needed. What ways can you make your wife feel attractive and sexy?

_____

_____

_____

_____

_____

_____

_____

_____

_____

_____

_____

_____

Let your wife be a fountain of blessing for you. Rejoice in the wife of your youth. She is a loving deer, a graceful doe. Let her breasts satisfy you always. May you always be captivated by her love.

Proverbs 5:18-19, NLT

Your kindness and tenderness will help your wife draw closer to you. Another issue is time. Actually spending time with her is important. Life is busy, and today society has people even busier than ever. However, you have to make a point to spend quality time with your wife. Nothing that I have spoken to you about concerning building emotional intimacy can be done without quality time. Just as you need to spend time in devotion, prayer and in the Word with the Lord, you need to spend time and devote yourself to your wife.

Devotion is a strong word. You should have devotion to God, as well as devotion to your wife. Devotion is defined as love, enthusiasm, and loyalty for a person. Your devotion to your wife is a spark to her love and enthusiasm for you. Conversely, disloyalty and betrayal will damage trust, communication, and ultimately your intimate relationship with your wife. I can't talk about sexual intimacy without talking about the importance of loyalty. Your marriage should be honored.

I know that this can be an area of struggle for men, but if you are committed to God and to your marriage, you will not defy this command. God calls you both to be loyal to each other. The enemy attacks this area heavily, and you must not give him room to move in this area of your life. There are things that you should know not to do so that you do not fall into temptation.

Does your wife feel your devotion? What can you do to demonstrate your devotion?

_____

_____

_____

_____

_____

_____

_____

_____

_____

_____

_____

_____

Give honor to marriage, and remain faithful to one another in marriage. God will surely judge people who are immoral and those who commit adultery.

Hebrews 13:4, NLT

Don't put yourself in situations or places that can be a cause of temptation. Carefully think about where you are going, who you surround yourself with, and what hobbies or habits that some may have that can cause you to stumble.

It is your responsibility to be mindful of what surroundings you expose yourself to. Don't think that you are strong enough to withhold from those types of temptations. It's not good to leave yourself vulnerable and uncovered. I am not saying that you are guaranteed to have any thoughts to betray your wife; but, this does not mean that you can be careless with this type of temptation.

Be careful what and who you are looking at. We have been using the construction as an analogy for your marriage. Well, when you are working in a construction project, you often wear protection goggles to protect your eyes. Protect your eyes from seeing things that can change your thoughts and lead you into sin.

Things such as pornography are harmful, and can ruin your mind and can give you a misconception of what your marriage bed should look like. It can damage your thinking concerning your sexual relationship with your wife. Your sexual connection with your wife is much deeper, and more profound than what you can find in a pornographic video. Although you may be in the actual physical sexual act with her, this can cause an emotional and spiritual disconnection with your wife. You are actually inviting the enemy into your bedroom when you invite the sexual thoughts and images you received through the pornography you watched.

Think about places you go, things you see, or conversations that you may put yourself in, that may be damaging to your personal relationship with the Lord and with your wife. List some ways that you can strategically avoid a way out of those situations.

_____

_____

_____

_____

_____

_____

_____

_____

_____

_____

_____

_____

But I say, anyone who even looks at a woman with lust has already committed adultery with her in his heart.

Matthew 5:28, NLT

Today, sources of pornography are not the only places we find the twisting and misconception of what God meant for sexual intimacy. Regular television and movies can also do that. You must make good judgment of what movies you expose yourself to seeing. If you have problems with pornography, you should first and foremost pray. You may need to consider seeking professional help, as well.

You are to do your best to avoid, and even run from sexual sin. It begins with a thought and it could lead to dangerous ground. Joseph (Genesis 37) is a great example. He ran as fast as he could and did not look back. So much so, that he left his shirt behind. Make sure that you are running from anything that can be a step into the direction of sexual sin.

Sex is only to be enjoyed in the confines of your marriage. Things such as infidelity and societal infiltrations about what sex should look like can cause harmful thoughts concerning sex. Sex was meant to be enjoyed, and was meant to be beautiful with your wife. Only with your wife, can you find and learn what God truly meant for you concerning sexual intimacy and pleasure.

God wants you to enjoy sex, but only with your wife. You should not be abstaining or withholding sex from each other unless it is by mutual agreement for health, or spiritual reasons like a fast. You both have the duty to fulfill each other's sexual needs.

Your wife should be your only link to sexual pleasure. Are you ensuring that your wife is your one and only? What areas can you discuss with your wife that has been difficult for you? Open discussion can be a way of running from temptation.

Run for sexual sin! No other sin so clearly affects the body as this one does. For sexual immorality is a sin against your own body.

1 Corinthians 6:18, NLT

Depriving each other is not healthy and gives room for the enemy to attack. This goes for both you and your wife. If you feel that your wife is abstaining from you, then you need to communicate that to her. It is important that you approach this carefully to see what the root problem is and resolve it.

Physical intimacy is important, but it isn't the most important part of your relationship. Your emotional intimacy is more important. The reason I say this is because if the day comes that due to illness one of you are unable to be intimate in that way, it is your deep connection with each other that will keep you together. The bond you have with each other and the Lord will see you through those times.

If either of you suffer from a health issue, make sure that you are communicating it with each other. Avoiding the conversation is not healthy. I understand that for men, it can be something very difficult to deal with, especially because our manhood is wrapped so much in our ability to please our wives. Sometimes, the issue can simply be stress related and the sharing can help. Alternatively, it may involve diet, sleep deprivation, or other things. Prayer, communication, and seeking the medical attention needed could help you make it through these types of situations.

You connect both physically and emotionally with physical intimacy. It can help draw you closer to one another, and help you show your wife how much you love her.

If there is an issue in the area of sexual intimacy, think about some things that may be the root cause. List and think about discussing with your wife.

_____

_____

_____

_____

_____

_____

_____

_____

Now regarding the questions you asked in your letter. Yes, it is good to abstain from sexual relations. But because there is so much sexual immorality, each man should have his own wife, and each woman should have her own husband. The husband should fulfill his wife's sexual needs, and the wife should fulfill her husband's needs. The wife gives authority over her body to her husband, and the husband gives authority over his body to his wife.

1 Corinthians 7:1-3, NLT

One of the things that you should do is initiate the occasion. It will make her feel attractive, beautiful, and desired. If you don't initiate physical intimacy, you could make her feel unattractive. Initiating an encounter can help your sexual intimacy to grow into becoming more sensational. However, for this you should be considerate of her physical needs. By this, I mean that you need to be a considerate lover. Make sure that you are doing your best to make her feel that your physical time together is about her and what she likes and needs.

Women are relational and inclusive, but this does not mean that they do not have physical desires. Her desires may be more romantic and more detailed. Take time to set the mood, and make her feel special, understood and cared for. Women desire passion.

Passion involves more than the act. Passion involves enthusiasm and excitement. Your marriage isn't a soap opera, but that doesn't mean that you can't be spontaneous once in a while.

Take her away, even if it is for one night. A time away from all the responsibilities to just relax and unwind can help your intimacy with each other. Surprise her with gifts of things she enjoys to do. My wife enjoys massages, so something that I could buy her is a certificate to get a massage. If money is tight, I can simply give her one myself. Passion doesn't necessarily always involve the actual act of sex. But, passion can certainly help.

Depriving each other is not good. However, if there is another issue, such as health or the like, make sure to discuss it with your wife. List some possible things you need to do to take out time to promote sexual intimacy with your wife.

Do not deprive each other of sexual relations, unless you both agree to refrain from sexual intimacy for a limited time so you can give yourselves more completely to prayer. Afterward, you should come together again so that Satan won't be able to tempt you because of your lack of self-control.

1 Corinthians 7:4-5, NLT

In Summary

In order for your home to look good, you have to make sure you take care of the decorating details inside. Make sure that you continue to build intimacy with God to help you deal with the things of your heart so that you are free to love your wife without reserve. Then make sure that you are spending time together with your wife in prayer and in the Word. Placing God in the center will help every area of your marriage including your intimate relationship with each other.

God cares about everything that we care about. He is our friend who understands us, and our needs. Seek an intimate and deeper relationship with him, and then seek an intimate and deeper relationship with your wife, and you will find that your marriage will be stronger than you ever imagined

Chapter Five - Discussion Questions

What are some things you would like to share with your wife regarding your intimate time together? How can you make her feel more loved and comfortable?

_____

_____

_____

_____

_____

_____

_____

_____

_____

_____

_____

_____

Chapter Five – Take Action!

Write a love letter to your wife. Express how much you appreciate her love for you; express what you find most attractive about her; express what her best character and physical features are.

_____

_____

_____

_____

_____

_____

_____

_____

_____

_____

_____

_____

_____

_____

Chapter 6

MAINTENANCE

...Look! I am placing a foundation stone...
...a precious cornerstone that is safe to build on....
Isaiah 28:16, NLT

We are finally here! You have reached the final stage of the construction project. However, the final stage can actually be one of the hardest. You have worked hard to get here. You have sought after the Lord, the Architect of this perfect plan, you made sure to lay the strongest foundation possible through communication with the Lord and your spouse. You then moved forward in identifying and learning your role so that you can perform the function that you, and only you were meant to do in this very special project.

The next step you took was not easy, but you did it, you worked together as a team and resolved conflict, and then you were able to have some fun together decorating this beautiful home through some intimate moments with the Lord and each other.

Now it's time for some maintenance. That's right, after you build something you have to maintain it. You want to make sure that what you built is built to last, and the way you do that is by making sure you maintain it. Making sure that you take care of what you put together. It can take lots of hard work, but by making sure you perform some preventative measures, you will not only ensure a life-long strong structure, but you will also make sure that it is here to last throughout generations after you.

When you build a home, you learn to love it more and more each day. But there will be challenges, and you must see through them. Just because you have done everything possible to make sure that everything in your home is perfect, doesn't mean that there won't be times that things go wrong. However, there are ways that you could do some preventative tasks in your home in order to minimize the work.

We have compared marriage relationships throughout this process to a construction project. This was something the Lord laid on my heart, and each step in the construction process is compared to real life marriages. In a real home, you might protect your foundation from damage by installing the correct gutters. You have to service your appliances, service any heating and plumbing systems, and apply fresh paint every now and then, etc.

One way love is demonstrated is through prayer, do you assure your spouse what you prayers are for them?

This is my commandment: Love each other in the same way I have loved you.

John 15:12, NLT

Keeping your Marriage Strong

So it is the same for your marriage. You have to make sure that you are protecting your relationship with God and each other, make sure that you are spending time with each other. Pray together, love each other, and stay committed. You do this through endurance and by being persistent in your intimacy with the Lord and each other. You do this by making sure that you are continuously working together to keep things going strong.

Even after you've worked on improving your marriage, you could still face tough times. You have learned some great ways to strengthen your marriage and to make it better than you could ever imagine. But this doesn't mean that it will be perfect. You still have to work and endure through everything together. Each challenge you face will make you stronger for the next.

Pray continuously for each other, and with each other. You have to be committed to growing spiritually. Even if it is only fifteen minutes a day, you should come together in prayer. You will find that your prayer time together will increase. If you find that you have missed a few days, there is no shame in starting the habit over. Just make sure that you are doing your best to have that moment of prayer.

You must make sacrifices in order to attain a deeper spiritual connection with the Lord. It's only through spiritual growth that

In what ways do you believe that you have grown as a couple?

_____

_____

_____

_____

_____

_____

_____

_____

_____

_____

_____

_____

_____

_____

Dear brothers and sisters, when troubles of any kind come your way, consider it an opportunity for great joy. For you know that when your faith is tested, your endurance has a chance to grow.
James 1:2-3, NLT

you'll be stronger each time you face another challenge. Remember that your marriage is made to reflect Christ and the Church, and you are not to follow the patterns of this world. Instead, know that the Lord who makes everything perfect designed your marriage.

When you are performing maintenance on something, you make sure to perform the required tasks according to the specifications of the instruction manual that came from the manufacturer. Well the Lord is our manufacturer, and His Word is the instruction manual. You need to stay plugged into His manual, and follow His instructions to the letter if you want everything to run smoothly.

Stay plugged into His Word; spend time in devotion with each other. Again, it doesn't have to be for hours. But you should be reading and sharing the Word together. If your spouse is having a difficult time with something, maybe work, with a friend, or anything, it is of great encouragement to give them scripture. I remember that there was a time that I was really going through a rough time, and Luis gave me a scripture that spoke directly to what I was going through. Not only was it helpful, but it brought me more appreciation for my husband because he took the time to look up a scripture that would be of an encouragement to me.

Just as if you would take thoughtful steps to ensure that things don't break down in a home, you should take thoughtful steps so that things don't break down with your spouse and their emotional

How can you sacrifice more time for your spouse?

_____

_____

_____

_____

_____

_____

_____

_____

_____

_____

_____

And so, dear brothers and sisters, I plead with you to give your bodies to God because of all he has done for you. Let them be a living and holy sacrifice—the kind he will find acceptable. This is truly the way to worship him. Don't copy the behavior and customs of this world, but let God transform you into a new person by changing the way you think. Then you will learn to know God's will for you, which is good and pleasing and perfect.

Romans 12:1-2, NLT

being. There are so many challenges that can face each of you individually that can then challenge the unit. Small considerations can make a world of difference.

Built to Last

Another thing is care. When you care for your home, you make sure to make the time to care for it. You have to make time for each other. Life is busy. Most homes have both spouses working in a career. Children can appear and take even more time. Then you have responsibilities with relatives, at church, and with friends. These can monopolize your time.

Life can sometimes get in the way. But, everything that can pull you away from each other will still be waiting even after you have sacrificed some time with each other. Make it a point to spend at least a few hours a week together alone just to relax and have fun. Make an appointment if you have to. It is definitely needed.

When you first got together, you probably tried to spend every waking moment together. It's time to go back to your first love. Remember your first love and take out time for each other. Ensuring that you are taking time to spend with each other cultivating your marriage is important. Second only to spending time with the Lord, this is one of the most important things you can do. Make sure to make plans for date night. Whether it is a night

Determine how you can make more time for God's Word.

_____

_____

_____

_____

_____

_____

_____

_____

_____

_____

_____

_____

_____

Your word is a lamp to guide my feet and a light for my path.
Psalms 119:105, NLT

on the town, or a quiet time alone at home, you need to take the time to be together. Take the time to talk, to laugh, and to share. This will strengthen your marriage.

Luis and I are not quite there yet, but soon we will be empty nesters. You may be going through this time right now. This time of your life is different, but I know that it can also be great. With children gone, so many thoughts and feelings can get in the way. Your children monopolized your time for so many years, that now you have to try to have other things to continue to connect you. This is where your intimate relationship and strong communication can help.

When it's just the two of you, whether it's new, or it has always been that way, you continually have to take time to cultivate your marriage. You want what you have built together to last a lifetime. The best way to do this is time. Whether you are newly married, or whether you have been married for years, time together will only build your marriage stronger. When moments get rough, the time you have spent together will help the rough times. When you are older, the amount of time you invested in your marriage is what is going to help you get through anything and keep your bond unbreakable.

I know that this can be difficult, and sometimes a challenge, but it is necessary. Many things can get in the way. Finances are one thing that can be a challenge, but there are free and other cost-efficient ways to spend time together. The important thing is that you both understand your finances, and plan with your budget in mind. However, I do suggest that every now and then you treat yourself in doing something you both really want and make the sacrifice to invest money into that time. It's an investment that you won't regret.

Another thing that comes against time, is time itself. Just because the years have set in and you are comfortable with each other doesn't mean that you can't try to be spontaneous every once in awhile. In a home, sometimes you do a makeover, and make changes to keep the home looking fresh and beautiful. Well, it's the same for your marriage. A fresh coat of paint, new curtains, and other touches make your home look great. Even if it's the same color of paint, your home can look brand new. Well, for your marriage it's the same.

Husbands, do something surprising for your wife. Just like the same paint, even if it's something that you've done for her when you were first together, you can make her happy. Wives, surprises are not only for husbands to do, you can certainly do something spontaneous for your husband. Small considerations go a long way. There is no shame in taking on the role of romancing your husband.

Try something new. New hobbies, and adventures can be helpful to build new memories. Sometimes holding on to the ways things used to be can be damaging. Don't get me wrong, it is great to remember the old times, and to re-live memories, but making new memories is even better. We all need times of fun and laughter. Times to try things that will spark up new interests. Building and rebuilding repeatedly is great.

Another helpful thing is to show interest in what your spouse has interest in. Luis loves sports. So, I often watch sports with him. This shows him that I care about what interests him. Luis does the same. He takes time to do things with me that I love. If your husband likes fishing, go fishing with him. If your wife likes romantic movies, watch them with her. I know some of these things may seem simple, but it is the simple things, that we can take for granted and pay no mind to its importance.

If one of you are the social bug and likes to entertain and invite friends over, then the other should be willing to have these times for the other. If it makes them happy, then go ahead and let them entertain. But, this also works in reverse. If one of you is not that social, then try to limit how often you entertain and have others over. Give and take. Don't confuse this with 50/50. This is actually 100/100.

You are both sacrificing fully in and every way possible for the interests of the other. Eventually this becomes continuous and should one day not be such a sacrifice. It would be nice for the time to come that you both enjoy the mere fact that you are making one another happy and content with the things that you do together.

I recall that when Luis and I were first married, he would stay in another room when I had people over. This would bother me so much. I felt that it was rude, and felt that it made people feel as though as they were not welcomed. I loved entertaining. I never fought with him about it.

When his family was over, I was tempted to do the same thing and kind of give him a taste of his own medicine, but I never did that. Instead, I acted with his family and friends the way I would have loved him to act when I had people over. I did communicate how I felt about it with him, and at first, he didn't do much to change. But as time passed, he started to do a bit more and more to be present when I had family or friends over.

As time passed, and as his relationship grew with the Lord, his love for people also began to grow. What's amazing is that today we are both the same in that respect. He also loves to entertain, and is often very considerate about the details of how we entertain. He wants to make people feel comfortable and at home. If he knows something about our guests, he makes sure to supply what they like for them when they are over, such as a favorite dessert, or a favorite game.

Luis did a total 180-degree turn. He is completely different. This is mainly because his relationship with the Lord helped his love for people grow, but also because he took the time to try to make me happy in this area. This is a great example of sacrificing something that eventually became joy and not such a sacrifice as well. Time and sacrifice will help your marriage last a lifetime.

Built to Last for your Children

You want your marriage to not only last throughout your lifetime, but also to be a testament of what God can do for generations to come. One way this happens is through your children, and through others. To be the prime example for your children, you can demonstrate a healthy, strong, God-filled, and God-inspired individual life and marriage.

Men, as the head of the household, you want to make sure that your children are staying grounded in the Word, and that they are learning to be fighters for their marriage. That they are learning to follow God's plan and design. You want your boys to follow your example to be a God-fearing husband and father. You want your grandchildren in the care of the best. Your sons should learn from you how to love God, how to lead their home, how to honor, trust, love and care for their wife, and how to love and care for their children. They should learn from you how to pray and keep their family united. But, best of all, how to keep their family in the Lord. So, when the time comes for your sons to begin a marital relationship, you know that you have armed them with the best lessons and tools to have a great marriage.

You are the first example for your sons. However, you are also the best example for your daughters as well. You will be showing your daughters what they are to look for in a husband by the way

In what ways can you sacrifice for the joy of your spouse?

...But as for me and my family, we will serve the Lord.
Joshua 24:15, NLT

you treat your wife. You are your daughters' first example of what a husband should do for her, the way a husband should act with her, and the way a husband should love her.

You want your daughters to be treated in the best way, so therefore you are to set that example by treating your wife the way you would want your daughters to be treated. Your daughters will know to look for a husband who will love her sacrificially, and who will love, trust, honor and respect her. There is a saying that daughter's will marry men like their fathers. Dad, you set the standard. How high would you set it when it concerns the future of your daughters?

Women, as the important helper, you too want to make sure that your children stay grounded in the Word. You want to nurture them, also show them to fight for their marriages. You are the first example to your daughters, and will show them what it is to be a Godly wife and mother.

Your daughters will learn from you how to establish and build their own homes through seeking wisdom from the Lord. Your daughters will learn about being grounded in the Word, and knowing their value in their relationships. They will know all that they need to know about strengthening their marriage through what you show them. They will learn how to teach and nurture their children as well.

You are also the first examples to your sons. You will show your sons what type of wife they should marry. You will show

What kind of example do you want to be? In what ways can you influence others?

...indeed, I have a beautiful inheritance.

Psalms 16:6, ESV

them how they should expect to be loved, honored and respected by their future wives. You are the first example of what type of wife they want to look for.

I am sure that you want your sons to be treated in the best way, so you set that example by treating your husband the way you would want your sons to be treated. Your sons will know to look for a wife who will love them sacrificially, and who will trust, honor and respect them. There is also a saying that sons will marry women like their mothers. Mom, you set the standard. How high would you set it when it concerns the future of your sons?

When you apply the Word of God in your marriage and do your best to live by it, you are not only saving your marriage, you are helping to establish a good foundation for the marriages of your children. You are placing in them the ability to distinguish between what the world has to say about marriage and what God says about marriage. You are allowing them to see that God's way is the best way, when you choose to make God's way the only way for your marriage. You are leaving them an inheritance that will be beautiful for you.

When your children go through challenges in their marriage, they will think about how you handled some of the same tough situations. You're ensuring that they will look for healthy relationships, and that they will seek after good counsel, including yours. Who better to advise your own children other than yourself? No other person cares for them, or wants better for them, than you.

Do you have healthy relationships with other couples? Name some that you may be interested in building a friendship, and then make a point to do it.

Remember the days of long ago; think about the generations past. Ask your father, and he will inform you. Inquire of your elders, and they will tell you.

Deuteronomy 32:7, NLT

It will bless you to know that not only did you do your best in your marriage and as parents, but that your best was acknowledged and was a good example for your children. Your children will know to seek your advice because of the example that you have given them. Then your children will influence their children and so forth. The life you lead in God now, will affect the generations to come. Raising children in a healthy environment will give them the best fighting chance at having future healthy families as well.

Built to Last as a Testament for Others

Another way that you will ensure that your testament will last past generations is your ability to affect other marriages as well. Through God, you can inspire your friends and their marriages. I have learned about breakups and divorces that have happened to good friends and it hurts when it happens.

But I have also seen Luis and I influence the marriages of other friends, and when we do, it is such a blessing to us that we were able to help. For me, this is a passion, and we want to see marriages changed near and far. It doesn't necessarily have to be a passion for you, but I am sure that you would love to positively affect the lives of those you care about and are close to you.

When you love Jesus and allow Him to reflect Himself in your marriage, you can affect others. You can testify to how Jesus has helped your marriage stay strong through the years by keeping him in the center. Throughout the years, Luis and I have always reached out to other couples. We try to spark a friendship and fellowship with them for a number of reasons. For one, we love people! We want to build relationship with people. It is so great to get to know other couples and hear their point of view and their stories.

It is good to find other Godly couples that you can bond with. It can be a great encouragement for your marriage. Good friendships help with stress, and help you grow your perspective with each other. When you are able to identify yourselves with other couples and see that you are normal with your issues, they become a little bit easier to face. You understand that you are not alone, that you are not the only couple that faces the types of challenges you face. This is important because a lie that the enemy often likes to use is that your relationship is in the worst shape, or that your relationship is abnormal, when in fact it's not.

Just like young children or teenagers, we also need to hang out with others. We laugh together and we learn from them just as much as they learn from us. This helps us in our marriage and it helps them. It is so great to bond with others that have the same faith, and are fighting the same battles. Don't be mistaken, most marriages face the same type of issues daily, and with good friendships you may not only help others, but you'll learn as well.

Conclusion

This has been quite a building project, and living out the information that you may have learned can help you tremendously. Keeping Christ in the center of your life, your marriage, and your family is the best action you can take. No one else can do for you as God does. But through that close relationship, change has to take hold of your life and you have to ensure that you are living an obedient life in the Lord. Obedience to His Word will lead you into the right path, and into the best life that you can possibly have.

Luis and I have tried our best to share with you all the concepts that we have learned through years of experience and straight from God's Word. This is because it is only through God's Word that you will live out the life and marriage that God intended for you. We challenge you today to put into practice the things we have shared with you in your marriage. We believe that when you do, you will not be disappointed.

Your marriage will be a marriage that was built to last!

Chapter Six - Discussion Questions

What are some things you could do for your wife, and places that you could go together, that she would enjoy?

_____

_____

_____

_____

_____

_____

_____

_____

_____

_____

_____

Chapter Six – Take Action!

Take some time to pray aloud together, expressing gratitude for specific things about each other that you're thankful for. Ask God to give you strength and wisdom to work on yourselves, both individually and as a couple. And Thank Him for the blessings in your marriage, both current, and those yet to come.

Final Assignment

Together with your wife, pick something to do, or a place to go from your list on page 217. Then make it happen!

_____

_____

_____

_____

_____

_____

_____

_____

_____

_____

_____

Find additional resources at **http://www.remodelministries.org**

Luis & Angela Hernandez, Remodel Ministries

Luis & Angela have a passion for carefully unpacking the truths of Scripture and the power of Scripture to change lives. They have served as leaders at Pleasant Valley Assembly of God for 10 years, in multiple ministries and capacities, including recently leading the local marriage ministry. They have been married for over 20 years, and have three children. They are passionate about ministering to marriages, writing, and teaching the Word of God. You can contact them at **angela@remodelministries.org**, or **luis@remodelministries.org**.

Made in the USA
Middletown, DE
19 April 2017